Resilience JOURNAL

DAILY REFLECTION
& SELF-CARE FOR
EDUCATORS

KAMI GUARINO

Resilience Journal: Daily Reflection & Self-Care for Educators

Published by Pontiac Way Publishing
Centennial, CO
info@PontiacWayPublishing.com

978-1-7329531-1-6
SELF-HELP / Journaling

Cover and Interior design by Victoria Wolf

QUANTITY PURCHASES: Schools, companies, professional groups, clubs, and other organizations may qualify for special terms when ordering quantities of this title. For information, email info@PontiacWayPublishing.com.

PONTIAC WAY
PUBLISHING

A school day can be crazy:

The highs and lows and wide-eyed flabbergasters—oftentimes all in the same day—can take their toll. As educators, we mentally and physically absorb that cumulative energy, and before we know it, that stress becomes all-consuming.

In the *Resilience Journal*, I have focused on three words that help shift an educator's mindset: **Listen, Relate, and Celebrate**. It's so simple yet such an oversight in our daily practice. As educators we chose this path to better the lives of others and make a positive impact. So often this intention is diverted by complacency, technical solutions, and noise. Commit to **listen, relate, and celebrate** the good in yourself and others, and not only will you feel a shift in your personal and professional space, but also you and your students will thrive and grow in more ways than you can imagine.

The *Resilience Journal* is a perfect way to navigate through your school days. It was created to emphasize the need for daily reflection and self-care for educators. Making this part of your routine is a daily reminder of your why and a tool that will help you stay focused, centered, and rooted in your passion to teach and lead.

I know educators don't need more to do! So I've structured the journal for you to practice self-care and so that you can reflect on your school day to maximize your effectiveness with minimal time used. When used daily, the journal will help bring clarity to who you are, what you need, and where you want to go. It will help you to gain perspective in challenging times, to celebrate the good, and to understand what's important to you.

Start your school day by setting your intention for a good day, releasing thoughts, feelings, or things that don't serve you, stating what you are thankful for, and focusing on only a few things that really matter. As your school day ends, reflect on your challenges and how well you were able to *listen, relate, celebrate,* and take care of yourself.

Be sure to check out and practice the daily mindful tips. These are some of my favorite practices that I have come across over the years. Research proves that mindfulness practice decreases stress and anxiety, increases attention, improves interpersonal relationships, strengthens compassion, and has many other wellness benefits.

If you had a difficult day, recognize it, be mindful, take a deep breath, reflect, and move on. Tomorrow is a new day!

It is time to thrive because you deserve it.
You've got this!

Tips for Using This Journal

Make it part of your daily routine. The more days you string together, the closer you are to forming a habit.

It's a new day.

MORNING PRACTICE

Today is a new day. Let's plan for a good one!

My INTENTION for today is . . .
Set your intention for a good day. What do you aim to do today?

I am THANKFUL for . . .
Incorporate daily gratitude. What are you thankful for? So often the small things in life get overlooked. Take time to claim what you are thankful for: a cup of coffee, the sun, your bed, a smile.

Navigate through the noise and simply FOCUS on three to-dos.
Deciding what to focus on helps set the goals and intentions for the day without all the noise attached to them. Avoid a huge to-do list by focusing like a laser beam on what really matters. If you do not get to all of them, tomorrow is another day!

Welcome today and RELEASE . . .
It is time to release. Releasing something that has consumed you in a negative way and no longer serves you allows you the space to be present and to focus on what matters today.

AFTERNOON PRACTICE

Reflect on how the day went.

Today I LISTENED to . . .
Reflect on what or who (it may be yourself) you listened to today. The more we listen, the better we respond to life.

Today I RELATED and CONNECTED to . . .
Did you connect with someone today? Were you able to strengthen a relation-ship? When we take time to connect to others and ourselves, we build trust, compassion, and empathy.

Today I CELEBRATED . . .
What went well today? There is always a silver lining in our day. Find it and write it down. It may be one good thing or many. Some days will be easier than others. Celebrate the people and things in your life.

What challenged me today and how can I shift my thinking?
Identify the challenge(s); reflect and think about whether there is anything you would do differently. Embrace challenges and look at them as an opportunity to move forward and thrive.

On a scale of one to ten, how did I do today?
At the end of the day, reflect and give yourself a number from one to ten repre-senting where you fall on the scale of surviving to thriving. Be honest with your-self so you can track patterns of barriers or builders to thrive.

SELF-CARE

I took care of myself today by . . .
Self-care is a key ingredient for being able to thrive. Commit to one self-care practice a day, even if it is only for ten minutes. You need to take care of yourself before you can take care of others. Self-care is the best gift to give yourself and your students!

Hydration is important.
Drinking eight glasses of water a day fires up your metabolism and increases your mental and physical performance throughout the day.

It's one hour before you go to bed.
Put your work aside (including your phone), breathe, and set your intention for tomorrow.

Here's a mindful tip.
Mindfully review your day. If the idea of being present is intriguing to you, then it's important to watch your progress, see what is working for you and what isn't, and challenge yourself to build your "mindfulness muscle" each and every day.

It's a new day!

TODAY'S MINDFUL TIP

Do you pay attention to your breathing? Practicing mindful, focused breathing, even for a few minutes a day, reduces stress and promotes relaxation. Before you get out of bed, bring your attention to your breathing. Observe five mindful breaths. Throughout the day, take a moment to focus on your breathing.

MORNING PRACTICE

My INTENTION for today is...
To listen more, talk less and be present
To not be so quick to judge

I am THANKFUL for...
The opportunity to be in front of kids everyday
My nice cup of coffee this morning
My health—I take it for granted sometimes

Navigate through the noise and simply FOCUS on three to-do's:

1 Stay on task and lean in during plan time

2 Morning Meeting with the kids to talk about empathy

3 Review essays and provide feedback

Welcome today and RELEASE....
The stress and struggle around the negativity of adult noise yesterday. Today I will start fresh!

AFTERNOON PRACTICE

I LISTENED to...

My students fears and worries about middle school
We had a great conversation!

I RELATED and CONNECTED to...

One of my parents who is frustrated with their child
My colleague who is struggling with change

I CELEBRATED...

With my class the growth they have made this week in
all areas. One of my students standing up for a
student they did not even know. A good day!

**What challenged me today and how can I shift my
thinking tomorrow?**

I felt that I was very ineffective working with one of my students that
was struggling today. Tomorrow I will focus more on what is going
right and where he is coming from instead of making it about me.

SELF CARE

I took care of myself today by...
Going to the gym and taking five minutes this
morning to take mindful breaths.

I drank 6 glasses of water today

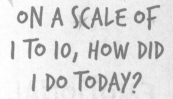

ON A SCALE OF
1 TO 10, HOW DID
I DO TODAY?

THRIVING 10

9

8

X

6

5

4

3

2

1 SURVIVING

Today I am at a 7

REMEMBER

An hour before I go to bed,
I will put my work aside
(and my phone), breathe
and set my intention for
tomorrow.

Resilience Reflection

EMOTIONAL RESILIENCE IS...

a person's ability to recover after a setback and to thrive in the midst of challenges, not just survive.

CHECK IN

Reflecting on the last 25 days, how well did I implement my daily practices (*before school, after school, self-care, mindfulness*)?

What went WELL?

I have made it a point to be present and practice mindfulness. I have focused more on what I can do and not necessarily what i have no control of. I definiately have made an effort to listen more and really understand where someone is coming from. Every day I tell my class we are in this together and we got this. Big win with one of my students: came to school for 4 weeks straight. He was really struggling with his attendance.

What did I STRUGGLE with?

Remaining asset focused. I got caught up in some adult drama. A couple of my kids' behavior in class. Reacting instead of putting the time in upfront to think out of the box of ways to address challenges.

ON ANY GIVEN DAY we experience a myriad of highs and lows. While some emotional resilience comes naturally to us, we all have the ability to increase our capacity over time and thrive.

Look back on the past 25 days. On a scale of 1 to 10, where do I FIND MYSELF on this line? *Add up your daily scores and divide by 25 to indicate your score.* I AM a ⬚7⬚

1 — 2 — 3 — 4 — 5 — 6 — ✗ — 8 — 9 — 10 →

SURVIVING   THRIVING

What ADJUSTMENTS can I make for the next 25 days to THRIVE?

Look for more moments to celebrate—big and small. Ask instead of assume. When struggling—look for solutions rather than focusing on the problem. Be able to recognize how I feel about a situation instead of assigning meaning to every little thing. Be the adult—our kids are looking at us everyday!

Keep Going!

You've Got This!

MY THOUGHTS TODAY...

Focus on the solution rather than the problem. When I get caught up in a problem and assign meaning to it—all it does is take time and energy away from moving forward.

I need to be decisive and look for ways to always connect with my kids.

I want to get a 10!

It's a new day!

TODAY'S MINDFUL TIP

Do you pay attention to your breathing? Practicing mindful, focused breathing, even for a few minutes a day, reduces stress and promotes relaxation. Before you get out of bed, bring your attention to your breathing. Observe five mindful breaths. Throughout the day, take a moment to focus on your breathing.

MORNING PRACTICE

My INTENTION for today is...

....

....

....

I am THANKFUL for...

....

....

....

Navigate through the noise and simply FOCUS on three to-do's:

1 ....

2 ....

3 ....

Welcome today and RELEASE....

....

....

....

AFTERNOON PRACTICE

I LISTENED to...

....

....

....

I RELATED and CONNECTED to...

....

....

....

I CELEBRATED...

....

....

....

What challenged me today and how can I shift my thinking tomorrow?

....

....

....

SELF CARE

I took care of myself today by...

....

....

....

I drank ☐ glasses of water today

ON A SCALE OF 1 TO 10, HOW DID I DO TODAY?

THRIVING 10
9
8
7
6
5
4
3
2
1 SURVIVING

Today I am at a ☐

REMEMBER

An hour before I go to bed, I will put my work aside (and my phone), breathe and set my intention for tomorrow.

It's a new day!

TODAY'S MINDFUL TIP

Take a few minutes today to go for a walk with open awareness. While staying connected to your breath, see how many colors, shapes, sounds, smells and sensations you notice. If you can't be outside, try walking around your home or school with an emphasis on seeing things in a new way.

MORNING PRACTICE

My INTENTION for today is...

....

....

....

I am THANKFUL for...

....

....

....

Navigate through the noise and simply FOCUS on three to-do's:

1 ....

2 ....

3 ....

Welcome today and RELEASE....

....

....

....

AFTERNOON PRACTICE

I LISTENED to...

....

....

....

I RELATED and CONNECTED to...

....

....

....

I CELEBRATED...

....

....

....

What challenged me today and how can I shift my thinking tomorrow?

....

....

....

SELF CARE

I took care of myself today by...

....

....

....

I drank ☐ glasses of water today

ON A SCALE OF 1 TO 10, HOW DID I DO TODAY?

THRIVING   10
           9
           8
           7
           6
           5
           4
           3
           2
           1   SURVIVING

Today I am at a ☐

REMEMBER

An hour before I go to bed, I will put my work aside (and my phone), breathe and set my intention for tomorrow.

It's a new day!

MORNING PRACTICE

My INTENTION for today is...

....
....
....

I am THANKFUL for...

....
....
....

Navigate through the noise and simply FOCUS on three to-do's:

1 ....

2 ....

3 ....

Welcome today and RELEASE....

....
....
....

TODAY'S MINDFUL TIP

Choosing to wake up a little earlier in the morning, not only allows you to begin your day with mindfulness, but also gives you more time to enjoy life. Give it a try for a week. You may be surprised at how much more you enjoy your mornings with just a few extra minutes.

AFTERNOON PRACTICE

I LISTENED to...

....

....

....

I RELATED and CONNECTED to...

....

....

....

I CELEBRATED...

....

....

....

What challenged me today and how can I shift my thinking tomorrow?

....

....

....

SELF CARE

I took care of myself today by...

....

....

....

I drank ☐ glasses of water today

ON A SCALE OF 1 TO 10, HOW DID I DO TODAY?

THRIVING 10
9
8
7
6
5
4
3
2
1 SURVIVING

Today I am at a ☐

REMEMBER

An hour before I go to bed, I will put my work aside (and my phone), breathe and set my intention for tomorrow.

DAY 4

It's a new day!

TODAY'S MINDFUL TIP

Take good things as gifts, not birthrights. Being grateful shuts the door on entitlement.

MORNING PRACTICE

My INTENTION for today is...

....

....

....

I am THANKFUL for...

....

....

....

Navigate through the noise and simply FOCUS on three to-do's:

1 ....

2 ....

3 ....

Welcome today and RELEASE....

....

....

....

AFTERNOON PRACTICE

I LISTENED to...

....

....

....

I RELATED and CONNECTED to...

....

....

....

I CELEBRATED...

....

....

....

What challenged me today and how can I shift my thinking tomorrow?

....

....

....

SELF CARE

I took care of myself today by...

....

....

....

I drank [   ] glasses of water today

ON A SCALE OF
1 TO 10, HOW DID
I DO TODAY?

THRIVING   10

9

8

7

6

5

4

3

2

1   SURVIVING

Today I am at a [   ]

REMEMBER

An hour before I go to bed, I will put my work aside (and my phone), breathe and set my intention for tomorrow.

It's a new day!

TODAY'S MINDFUL TIP

"Mindfulness is simply being aware of what is happening right now without wishing it were different; enjoying the pleasant without holding on when it changes (which it will); being with the unpleasant without fearing it will always be this way (which it won't)."

~James Baraz

MORNING PRACTICE

My INTENTION for today is...

....
....
....

I am THANKFUL for...

....
....
....

Navigate through the noise and simply FOCUS on three to-do's:

1 ....

2 ....

3 ....

Welcome today and RELEASE....

....
....
....

AFTERNOON PRACTICE

I LISTENED to...

_____

_____

_____

I RELATED and CONNECTED to...

_____

_____

_____

I CELEBRATED...

_____

_____

_____

What challenged me today and how can I shift my thinking tomorrow?

_____

_____

_____

SELF CARE

I took care of myself today by...

_____

_____

_____

I drank ☐ glasses of water today

ON A SCALE OF 1 TO 10, HOW DID I DO TODAY?

THRIVING 10
9
8
7
6
5
4
3
2
1 SURVIVING

Today I am at a ☐

REMEMBER

An hour before I go to bed, I will put my work aside (and my phone), breathe and set my intention for tomorrow.

It's a new day!

TODAY'S MINDFUL TIP

Check in with someone you have not spoken with recently. You will feel good for nurturing the connection and who knows, your thoughtfulness might just be the boost they needed to get through the day.

MORNING PRACTICE

My INTENTION for today is...

....

....

....

I am THANKFUL for...

....

....

....

Navigate through the noise and simply FOCUS on three to-do's:

1 ....

2 ....

3 ....

Welcome today and RELEASE....

....

....

....

AFTERNOON PRACTICE

I LISTENED to...

_____

_____

_____

I RELATED and CONNECTED to...

_____

_____

_____

I CELEBRATED...

_____

_____

_____

What challenged me today and how can I shift my thinking tomorrow?

_____

_____

_____

SELF CARE

I took care of myself today by...

_____

_____

_____

I drank ☐ glasses of water today

ON A SCALE OF 1 TO 10, HOW DID I DO TODAY?

THRIVING 10

9

8

7

6

5

4

3

2

1 SURVIVING

Today I am at a ☐

REMEMBER

An hour before I go to bed, I will put my work aside (and my phone), breathe and set my intention for tomorrow.

DAY 7

It's a new day!

TODAY'S MINDFUL TIP

Think of a word/feeling you would like to **embrace** and think of a word/feeling you would like to **let go of**. As you inhale, silently say to yourself the word you'd like to embrace and as you exhale, silently say to yourself the word you'd like to release.

MORNING PRACTICE

My INTENTION for today is...

....

....

....

I am THANKFUL for...

....

....

....

Navigate through the noise and simply FOCUS on three to-do's:

1 ....

2 ....

3 ....

Welcome today and RELEASE....

....

....

....

AFTERNOON PRACTICE

I LISTENED to...

....

....

....

I RELATED and CONNECTED to...

....

....

....

I CELEBRATED...

....

....

....

What challenged me today and how can I shift my thinking tomorrow?

....

....

....

SELF CARE

I took care of myself today by...

....

....

....

I drank ☐ glasses of water today

ON A SCALE OF
1 TO 10, HOW DID
I DO TODAY?

THRIVING 10

9

8

7

6

5

4

3

2

1 SURVIVING

Today I am at a ☐

REMEMBER

An hour before I go to bed, I will put my work aside (and my phone), breathe and set my intention for tomorrow.

It's a new day!

TODAY'S
MINDFUL TIP

Instead of adding fuel to the fire, water it with pure goodness.

MORNING PRACTICE

My INTENTION for today is...

....
....
....

I am THANKFUL for...

....
....
....

Navigate through the noise and simply FOCUS on three to-do's:

1 ....

2 ....

3 ....

Welcome today and RELEASE....

....
....
....

AFTERNOON PRACTICE

I LISTENED to...

_____

_____

_____

I RELATED and CONNECTED to...

_____

_____

_____

I CELEBRATED...

_____

_____

_____

What challenged me today and how can I shift my thinking tomorrow?

_____

_____

_____

SELF CARE

I took care of myself today by...

_____

_____

_____

I drank ☐ glasses of water today

ON A SCALE OF 1 TO 10, HOW DID I DO TODAY?

THRIVING 10

9

8

7

6

5

4

3

2

1 SURVIVING

Today I am at a ☐

REMEMBER

An hour before I go to bed, I will put my work aside (and my phone), breathe and set my intention for tomorrow.

It's a new day!

MORNING PRACTICE

My INTENTION for today is...

....

....

....

I am THANKFUL for...

....

....

....

Navigate through the noise and simply FOCUS on three to-do's:

1 ....

2 ....

3 ....

Welcome today and RELEASE....

....

....

....

AFTERNOON PRACTICE

I LISTENED to...

....

....

....

I RELATED and CONNECTED to...

....

....

....

I CELEBRATED...

....

....

....

What challenged me today and how can I shift my thinking tomorrow?

....

....

....

SELF CARE

I took care of myself today by...

....

....

....

I drank ☐ glasses of water today

ON A SCALE OF 1 TO 10, HOW DID I DO TODAY?

↑

THRIVING 10

9

8

7

6

5

4

3

2

1 SURVIVING

Today I am at a ☐

REMEMBER

An hour before I go to bed, I will put my work aside (and my phone), breathe and set my intention for tomorrow.

It's a new day!

MORNING PRACTICE

My INTENTION for today is...

....

....

....

I am THANKFUL for...

....

....

....

Navigate through the noise and simply FOCUS on three to-do's:

1 ....

2 ....

3 ....

Welcome today and RELEASE....

....

....

....

TODAY'S MINDFUL TIP

Do one thing today that you have been putting off. Embrace the satisfaction of checking it off your list.

AFTERNOON PRACTICE

I LISTENED to...

....

....

....

I RELATED and CONNECTED to...

....

....

....

I CELEBRATED...

....

....

....

What challenged me today and how can I shift my thinking tomorrow?

....

....

....

SELF CARE

I took care of myself today by...

....

....

....

I drank ☐ glasses of water today

ON A SCALE OF 1 TO 10, HOW DID I DO TODAY?

THRIVING 10

9

8

7

6

5

4

3

2

1 SURVIVING

Today I am at a ☐

REMEMBER

An hour before I go to bed, I will put my work aside (and my phone), breathe and set my intention for tomorrow.

It's a new day!

TODAY'S MINDFUL TIP

A Personal Life Vision can help frame your life, point you in the right direction to help achieve your goals, and act as a tool to remind you of your primary concerns. For the next five days I will ask you a question to help create this.

Personal Life Vision question one: What things do you stand for? Jot them down below.

MORNING PRACTICE

My INTENTION for today is...

....

....

....

I am THANKFUL for...

....

....

....

Navigate through the noise and simply FOCUS on three to-do's:

1 ....

2 ....

3 ....

Welcome today and RELEASE....

....

....

....

AFTERNOON PRACTICE

I LISTENED to...

_____

_____

_____

I RELATED and CONNECTED to...

_____

_____

_____

I CELEBRATED...

_____

_____

_____

What challenged me today and how can I shift my thinking tomorrow?

_____

_____

_____

SELF CARE

I took care of myself today by...

_____

_____

_____

I drank ☐ glasses of water today

ON A SCALE OF 1 TO 10, HOW DID I DO TODAY?

THRIVING 10

9

8

7

6

5

4

3

2

1 SURVIVING

Today I am at a ☐

REMEMBER

An hour before I go to bed, I will put my work aside (and my phone), breathe and set my intention for tomorrow.

It's a new day!

MORNING PRACTICE

My INTENTION for today is...

....

....

....

I am THANKFUL for...

....

....

....

Navigate through the noise and simply FOCUS on three to-do's:

1 ....

2 ....

3 ....

Welcome today and RELEASE....

....

....

....

AFTERNOON PRACTICE

I LISTENED to...

....

....

....

I RELATED and CONNECTED to...

....

....

....

I CELEBRATED...

....

....

....

What challenged me today and how can I shift my thinking tomorrow?

....

....

....

SELF CARE

I took care of myself today by...

....

....

....

I drank ☐ glasses of water today

ON A SCALE OF I TO 10, HOW DID I DO TODAY?

THRIVING 10

9

8

7

6

5

4

3

2

1 SURVIVING

Today I am at a ☐

REMEMBER

An hour before I go to bed, I will put my work aside (and my phone), breathe and set my intention for tomorrow.

It's a new day!

TODAY'S MINDFUL TIP

Personal Life Vision question three:
How do you want to live your life? Jot it down below.

MORNING PRACTICE

My INTENTION for today is...

....

....

....

I am THANKFUL for...

....

....

....

Navigate through the noise and simply FOCUS on three to-do's:

1 ....

2 ....

3 ....

Welcome today and RELEASE....

....

....

....

AFTERNOON PRACTICE

I LISTENED to...

....

....

....

I RELATED and CONNECTED to...

....

....

....

I CELEBRATED...

....

....

....

What challenged me today and how can I shift my thinking tomorrow?

....

....

....

SELF CARE

I took care of myself today by...

....

....

....

I drank ☐ glasses of water today

ON A SCALE OF 1 TO 10, HOW DID I DO TODAY?

THRIVING 10
9
8
7
6
5
4
3
2
1 SURVIVING

Today I am at a ☐

REMEMBER

An hour before I go to bed, I will put my work aside (and my phone), breathe and set my intention for tomorrow.

It's a new day!

TODAY'S MINDFUL TIP

Personal Life Vision questions four:
How do you want to define yourself? Jot it down below.

MORNING PRACTICE

My INTENTION for today is...

....
....
....

I am THANKFUL for...

....
....
....

Navigate through the noise and simply FOCUS on three to-do's:

1 ....

2 ....

3 ....

Welcome today and RELEASE....

....
....
....

AFTERNOON PRACTICE

I LISTENED to...

....

....

....

I RELATED and CONNECTED to...

....

....

....

I CELEBRATED...

....

....

....

What challenged me today and how can I shift my thinking tomorrow?

....

....

....

SELF CARE

I took care of myself today by...

....

....

....

I drank ☐ glasses of water today

ON A SCALE OF 1 TO 10, HOW DID I DO TODAY?

THRIVING 10

9

8

7

6

5

4

3

2

1 SURVIVING

Today I am at a ☐

REMEMBER

An hour before I go to bed, I will put my work aside (and my phone), breathe and set my intention for tomorrow.

DAY 15

It's a new day!

TODAY'S MINDFUL TIP

Personal Life Vision question five:
What words do you want to live by? Jot them down below.

Put the last five days of responses together and make it visible to you. A Personal Life Vision can be a powerful tool for bringing about your best life. Refer to your Personal Life Vision often.

MORNING PRACTICE

My INTENTION for today is...

....

....

....

I am THANKFUL for...

....

....

....

Navigate through the noise and simply FOCUS on three to-do's:

1 ....

2 ....

3 ....

Welcome today and RELEASE....

....

....

....

AFTERNOON PRACTICE

I LISTENED to...

....

....

....

I RELATED and CONNECTED to...

....

....

....

I CELEBRATED...

....

....

....

What challenged me today and how can I shift my thinking tomorrow?

....

....

....

SELF CARE

I took care of myself today by...

....

....

I drank ☐ glasses of water today

ON A SCALE OF 1 TO 10, HOW DID I DO TODAY?

THRIVING 10
9
8
7
6
5
4
3
2
1 SURVIVING

Today I am at a ☐

REMEMBER

An hour before I go to bed, I will put my work aside (and my phone), breathe and set my intention for tomorrow.

It's a new day!

TODAY'S
MINDFUL TIP

"What day is it?" asked Pooh. "It's today," squeaked Piglet. "My favorite day," said Pooh.

MORNING PRACTICE

My INTENTION for today is...

....

....

....

I am THANKFUL for...

....

....

....

Navigate through the noise and simply FOCUS on three to-do's:

1 ....

2 ....

3 ....

Welcome today and RELEASE....

....

....

....

AFTERNOON PRACTICE

I LISTENED to...

_____

_____

_____

I RELATED and CONNECTED to...

_____

_____

_____

I CELEBRATED...

_____

_____

_____

What challenged me today and how can I shift my thinking tomorrow?

_____

_____

_____

SELF CARE

I took care of myself today by...

_____

_____

_____

I drank [ ] glasses of water today

ON A SCALE OF 1 TO 10, HOW DID I DO TODAY?

THRIVING 10

9

8

7

6

5

4

3

2

1 SURVIVING

Today I am at a [ ]

REMEMBER

An hour before I go to bed, I will put my work aside (and my phone), breathe and set my intention for tomorrow.

It's a new day!

TODAY'S MINDFUL TIP

Have a dance party. Be goofy and get your heart rate up at the same time.

MORNING PRACTICE

My INTENTION for today is...

....

....

....

I am THANKFUL for...

....

....

....

Navigate through the noise and simply FOCUS on three to-do's:

1 ....

2 ....

3 ....

Welcome today and RELEASE....

....

....

....

AFTERNOON PRACTICE

I LISTENED to...

....

....

....

I RELATED and CONNECTED to...

....

....

....

I CELEBRATED...

....

....

....

What challenged me today and how can I shift my thinking tomorrow?

....

....

....

SELF CARE

I took care of myself today by...

....

....

....

I drank ☐ glasses of water today

ON A SCALE OF 1 TO 10, HOW DID I DO TODAY?

THRIVING 10

9

8

7

6

5

4

3

2

1 SURVIVING

Today I am at a ☐

REMEMBER

An hour before I go to bed, I will put my work aside (and my phone), breathe and set my intention for tomorrow.

It's a new day!

TODAY'S MINDFUL TIP

Reconnect: When it comes down to it, our relationships are one of the few things that really matter. It is never too late to reconnect with your loved ones. You are strengthening bonds that will allow you to look back on your life with gratitude rather than regret.

MORNING PRACTICE

My INTENTION for today is...

....

....

....

I am THANKFUL for...

....

....

....

Navigate through the noise and simply FOCUS on three to-do's:

1 ....

2 ....

3 ....

Welcome today and RELEASE....

....

....

....

AFTERNOON PRACTICE

I LISTENED to...

....

....

....

I RELATED and CONNECTED to...

....

....

....

I CELEBRATED...

....

....

....

What challenged me today and how can I shift my thinking tomorrow?

....

....

....

SELF CARE

I took care of myself today by...

....

....

....

I drank ☐ glasses of water today

ON A SCALE OF 1 TO 10, HOW DID I DO TODAY?

THRIVING 10
9
8
7
6
5
4
3
2
1 SURVIVING

Today I am at a ☐

REMEMBER

An hour before I go to bed, I will put my work aside (and my phone), breathe and set my intention for tomorrow.

It's a new day!

MORNING PRACTICE

My INTENTION for today is...

....

....

....

I am THANKFUL for...

....

....

....

Navigate through the noise and simply FOCUS on three to-do's:

1 ....

2 ....

3 ....

Welcome today and RELEASE....

....

....

....

AFTERNOON PRACTICE

I LISTENED to...

_____

_____

_____

I RELATED and CONNECTED to...

_____

_____

_____

I CELEBRATED...

_____

_____

_____

What challenged me today and how can I shift my
thinking tomorrow?

_____

_____

_____

SELF CARE

I took care of myself today by...

_____

_____

_____

I drank ☐ glasses of water today

ON A SCALE OF
1 TO 10, HOW DID
I DO TODAY?

THRIVING 10
9
8
7
6
5
4
3
2
1 SURVIVING

Today I am at a ☐

REMEMBER

An hour before I go to bed,
I will put my work aside
(and my phone), breathe
and set my intention for
tomorrow.

It's a new day!

TODAY'S MINDFUL TIP

Let those we listen to know we are paying attention and thinking about what they shared. We do this by maintaining eye contact, nodding, smiling and encouraging them to express their thoughts.

MORNING PRACTICE

My INTENTION for today is...

....

....

....

I am THANKFUL for...

....

....

....

Navigate through the noise and simply FOCUS on three to-do's:

1 ....

2 ....

3 ....

Welcome today and RELEASE....

....

....

....

AFTERNOON PRACTICE

I LISTENED to...

_____

_____

_____

I RELATED and CONNECTED to...

_____

_____

_____

I CELEBRATED...

_____

_____

_____

What challenged me today and how can I shift my thinking tomorrow?

_____

_____

_____

SELF CARE

I took care of myself today by...

_____

_____

_____

I drank ☐ glasses of water today

ON A SCALE OF 1 TO 10, HOW DID I DO TODAY?

THRIVING 10
9
8
7
6
5
4
3
2
1 SURVIVING

Today I am at a ☐

REMEMBER

An hour before I go to bed, I will put my work aside (and my phone), breathe and set my intention for tomorrow.

It's a new day!

TODAY'S MINDFUL TIP

When you find yourself taking a good thing for granted, think about life without it. Contemplating not having something you care about makes you more grateful for the life you currently have.

MORNING PRACTICE

My INTENTION for today is...

....
....
....

I am THANKFUL for...

....
....
....

Navigate through the noise and simply FOCUS on three to-do's:

1 ....

2 ....

3 ....

Welcome today and RELEASE....

....
....
....

AFTERNOON PRACTICE

I LISTENED to...

....
....
....

I RELATED and CONNECTED to...

....
....
....

I CELEBRATED...

....
....
....

What challenged me today and how can I shift my thinking tomorrow?

....
....
....

SELF CARE

I took care of myself today by...

....
....
....

I drank ☐ glasses of water today

ON A SCALE OF 1 TO 10, HOW DID I DO TODAY?

THRIVING 10
9
8
7
6
5
4
3
2
1 SURVIVING

Today I am at a ☐

REMEMBER

An hour before I go to bed, I will put my work aside (and my phone), breathe and set my intention for tomorrow.

It's a new day!

MORNING PRACTICE

My INTENTION for today is...

....

....

....

I am THANKFUL for...

....

....

....

Navigate through the noise and simply FOCUS on three to-do's:

1 ....

2 ....

3 ....

Welcome today and RELEASE....

....

....

....

AFTERNOON PRACTICE

I LISTENED to...

....

....

....

I RELATED and CONNECTED to...

....

....

....

I CELEBRATED...

....

....

....

What challenged me today and how can I shift my thinking tomorrow?

....

....

....

SELF CARE

I took care of myself today by...

....

....

....

I drank ⬜ glasses of water today

ON A SCALE OF 1 TO 10, HOW DID I DO TODAY?

THRIVING 10
9
8
7
6
5
4
3
2
1 SURVIVING

Today I am at a ⬜

REMEMBER

An hour before I go to bed, I will put my work aside (and my phone), breathe and set my intention for tomorrow.

It's a new day!

MORNING PRACTICE

My INTENTION for today is...

....
....
....

I am THANKFUL for...

....
....
....

Navigate through the noise and simply FOCUS on three to-do's:

1 ....

2 ....

3 ....

Welcome today and RELEASE....

....
....
....

AFTERNOON PRACTICE

I LISTENED to...

....

....

....

I RELATED and CONNECTED to...

....

....

....

I CELEBRATED...

....

....

....

What challenged me today and how can I shift my thinking tomorrow?

....

....

....

SELF CARE

I took care of myself today by...

....

....

....

I drank ☐ glasses of water today

ON A SCALE OF 1 TO 10, HOW DID I DO TODAY?

THRIVING 10

9

8

7

6

5

4

3

2

1 SURVIVING

Today I am at a ☐

REMEMBER

An hour before I go to bed, I will put my work aside (and my phone), breathe and set my intention for tomorrow.

It's a new day!

MORNING PRACTICE

My INTENTION for today is...

....

....

....

I am THANKFUL for...

....

....

....

Navigate through the noise and simply FOCUS on three to-do's:

1 ....

2 ....

3 ....

Welcome today and RELEASE....

....

....

....

TODAY'S MINDFUL TIP

Grateful people are specific: When you tell someone specifically why you are grateful, it makes it personal and authentic. It shows that you are genuinely paying attention, caring and investing in them.

AFTERNOON PRACTICE

I LISTENED to...

....

....

....

I RELATED and CONNECTED to...

....

....

....

I CELEBRATED...

....

....

....

What challenged me today and how can I shift my thinking tomorrow?

....

....

SELF CARE

I took care of myself today by...

....

....

I drank ☐ glasses of water today

ON A SCALE OF
1 TO 10, HOW DID
I DO TODAY?

THRIVING 10

9

8

7

6

5

4

3

2

1 SURVIVING

Today I am at a ☐

REMEMBER
An hour before I go to bed,
I will put my work aside
(and my phone), breathe
and set my intention for
tomorrow.

Resilience Reflection

EMOTIONAL RESILIENCE IS...

a person's ability to recover after a setback and to thrive in the midst of challenges, not just survive.

CHECK IN

Reflecting on the last 25 days, how well did I implement my daily practices (*before school, after school, self-care, mindfulness*)?

What went WELL?

....

....

....

....

What did I STRUGGLE with?

....

....

....

....

ON ANY GIVEN DAY we experience a myriad of highs and lows. While some emotional resilience comes naturally to us, we all have the ability to increase our capacity over time and thrive.

Look back on the past 25 days. On a scale of 1 to 10, where do I **FIND MYSELF** on this line? *Add up your daily scores and divide by 25 to indicate your score.* I AM a ☐

1   2   3   4   5   6   7   8   9   10 →

SURVIVING   THRIVING

What **ADJUSTMENTS** can I make for the next 25 days to **THRIVE**?

....

....

....

....

Keep Going!

You've Got This!

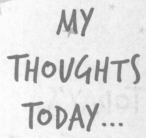

TODAY'S MINDFUL TIP

Smile in the Mirror:
Although it seems silly, smiling at yourself in the mirror first thing in the morning has many positive benefits for your well-being.

It's a new day!

MORNING PRACTICE

My INTENTION for today is...

....

....

....

I am THANKFUL for...

....

....

....

Navigate through the noise and simply FOCUS on three to-do's:

1 ....

2 ....

3 ....

Welcome today and RELEASE....

....

....

....

AFTERNOON PRACTICE

I LISTENED to...

....

....

....

I RELATED and CONNECTED to...

....

....

....

I CELEBRATED...

....

....

....

What challenged me today and how can I shift my thinking tomorrow?

....

....

....

SELF CARE

I took care of myself today by...

....

....

....

I drank ☐ glasses of water today

ON A SCALE OF
I TO 10, HOW DID
I DO TODAY?

THRIVING 10

9

8

7

6

5

4

3

2

1 SURVIVING

Today I am at a ☐

REMEMBER

An hour before I go to bed,
I will put my work aside
(and my phone), breathe
and set my intention for
tomorrow.

It's a new day!

MORNING PRACTICE

My INTENTION for today is...

....

....

....

I am THANKFUL for...

....

....

....

Navigate through the noise and simply FOCUS on three to-do's:

1 ....

2 ....

3 ....

Welcome today and RELEASE....

....

....

....

TODAY'S MINDFUL TIP

Go the entire day without complaining. So simple but yet difficult. Retrain your brain and prune those negative neuron connections that no longer serve you.

AFTERNOON PRACTICE

I LISTENED to...

....

....

....

I RELATED and CONNECTED to...

....

....

....

I CELEBRATED...

....

....

....

What challenged me today and how can I shift my thinking tomorrow?

....

....

....

SELF CARE

I took care of myself today by...

....

....

....

I drank ☐ glasses of water today

ON A SCALE OF 1 TO 10, HOW DID I DO TODAY?

THRIVING 10
9
8
7
6
5
4
3
2
1 SURVIVING

Today I am at a ☐

REMEMBER

An hour before I go to bed, I will put my work aside (and my phone), breathe and set my intention for tomorrow.

It's a new day!

MORNING PRACTICE

My INTENTION for today is...

....

....

....

I am THANKFUL for...

....

....

....

Navigate through the noise and simply FOCUS on three to-do's:

1 ....

2 ....

3 ....

Welcome today and RELEASE....

....

....

....

AFTERNOON PRACTICE

I LISTENED to...

....

....

....

I RELATED and CONNECTED to...

....

....

....

I CELEBRATED...

....

....

....

What challenged me today and how can I shift my thinking tomorrow?

....

....

....

SELF CARE

I took care of myself today by...

....

....

....

I drank ☐ glasses of water today

ON A SCALE OF 1 TO 10, HOW DID I DO TODAY?

THRIVING 10

9

8

7

6

5

4

3

2

1 SURVIVING

Today I am at a ☐

REMEMBER

An hour before I go to bed, I will put my work aside (and my phone), breathe and set my intention for tomorrow.

It's a new day!

TODAY'S MINDFUL TIP

When you're feeling depleted, take a moment and write down some things that spark gratitude in you.

MORNING PRACTICE

My INTENTION for today is...

....

....

....

I am THANKFUL for...

....

....

....

Navigate through the noise and simply FOCUS on three to-do's:

1 ....

2 ....

3 ....

Welcome today and RELEASE....

....

....

....

AFTERNOON PRACTICE

I LISTENED to...

....

....

....

I RELATED and CONNECTED to...

....

....

....

I CELEBRATED...

....

....

....

What challenged me today and how can I shift my thinking tomorrow?

....

....

....

SELF CARE

I took care of myself today by...

....

....

I drank ☐ glasses of water today

ON A SCALE OF 1 TO 10, HOW DID I DO TODAY?

THRIVING 10

9

8

7

6

5

4

3

2

1 SURVIVING

Today I am at a ☐

REMEMBER

An hour before I go to bed, I will put my work aside (and my phone), breathe and set my intention for tomorrow.

It's a new day!

TODAY'S MINDFUL TIP

THINK

Think outside the box.

Honor those around you.

Ignite a shift.

Never settle for the status quo.

Kindness goes a long way.

MORNING PRACTICE

My INTENTION for today is...

....

....

....

I am THANKFUL for...

....

....

....

Navigate through the noise and simply FOCUS on three to-do's:

1 ....

2 ....

3 ....

Welcome today and RELEASE....

....

....

....

AFTERNOON PRACTICE

I LISTENED to...

....

....

....

I RELATED and CONNECTED to...

....

....

....

I CELEBRATED...

....

....

....

What challenged me today and how can I shift my thinking tomorrow?

....

....

....

SELF CARE

I took care of myself today by...

....

....

....

I drank ☐ glasses of water today

ON A SCALE OF 1 TO 10, HOW DID I DO TODAY?

THRIVING 10
9
8
7
6
5
4
3
2
1 SURVIVING

Today I am at a ☐

REMEMBER

An hour before I go to bed, I will put my work aside (and my phone), breathe and set my intention for tomorrow.

It's a new day!

MORNING PRACTICE

My INTENTION for today is...

....

....

....

I am THANKFUL for...

....

....

....

Navigate through the noise and simply FOCUS on three to-do's:

1 ....

2 ....

3 ....

Welcome today and RELEASE....

....

....

....

TODAY'S MINDFUL TIP

Describe in detail how your body feels when you express gratitude. What kinds of thoughts and emotions do you notice? When you turn more towards things you appreciate, your days are that much better.

AFTERNOON PRACTICE

I LISTENED to...

....

....

....

I RELATED and CONNECTED to...

....

....

....

I CELEBRATED...

....

....

....

What challenged me today and how can I shift my thinking tomorrow?

....

....

....

SELF CARE

I took care of myself today by...

....

....

....

I drank ☐ glasses of water today

ON A SCALE OF 1 TO 10, HOW DID I DO TODAY?

THRIVING 10
9
8
7
6
5
4
3
2
1 SURVIVING

Today I am at a ☐

REMEMBER

An hour before I go to bed, I will put my work aside (and my phone), breathe and set my intention for tomorrow.

It's a new day!

Challenge: It's easy to be thankful for the good. Try and be thankful for the "not so good". Realize the power you have to transform an obstacle into an opportunity.

MORNING PRACTICE

My INTENTION for today is...

....

....

....

I am THANKFUL for...

....

....

....

Navigate through the noise and simply FOCUS on three to-do's:

1 ....

2 ....

3 ....

Welcome today and RELEASE....

....

....

....

AFTERNOON PRACTICE

I LISTENED to...

....

....

....

I RELATED and CONNECTED to...

....

....

....

I CELEBRATED...

....

....

....

What challenged me today and how can I shift my thinking tomorrow?

....

....

....

SELF CARE

I took care of myself today by...

....

....

....

I drank [ ] glasses of water today

ON A SCALE OF 1 TO 10, HOW DID I DO TODAY?

THRIVING 10
9
8
7
6
5
4
3
2
1 SURVIVING

Today I am at a [ ]

REMEMBER

An hour before I go to bed, I will put my work aside (and my phone), breathe and set my intention for tomorrow.

DAY 33

It's a new day!

TODAY'S MINDFUL TIP

The simplest way to get in touch with how you're feeling is to do a **mindful body scan**. Get comfortable and bring your attention to every area of your body beginning at the toes and moving to the head. Pause at each part for a moment and pay close attention to how you feel.

MORNING PRACTICE

My INTENTION for today is...

....

....

....

I am THANKFUL for...

....

....

....

Navigate through the noise and simply FOCUS on three to-do's:

1 ....

2 ....

3 ....

Welcome today and RELEASE....

....

....

....

AFTERNOON PRACTICE

I LISTENED to...

....

....

....

I RELATED and CONNECTED to...

....

....

....

I CELEBRATED...

....

....

....

What challenged me today and how can I shift my thinking tomorrow?

....

....

....

SELF CARE

I took care of myself today by...

....

....

....

I drank ☐ glasses of water today

ON A SCALE OF
I TO 10, HOW DID
I DO TODAY?

THRIVING   10
9
8
7
6
5
4
3
2
1   SURVIVING

Today I am at a ☐

REMEMBER

An hour before I go to bed,
I will put my work aside
(and my phone), breathe
and set my intention for
tomorrow.

It's a new day!

TODAY'S MINDFUL TIP

Power Up: Look in the mirror and strike a power pose. A reminder that you hold the power to all possibilities.

MORNING PRACTICE

My INTENTION for today is...

....

....

....

I am THANKFUL for...

....

....

....

Navigate through the noise and simply FOCUS on three to-do's:

1 ....

2 ....

3 ....

Welcome today and RELEASE....

....

....

....

AFTERNOON PRACTICE

I LISTENED to...

....

....

....

I RELATED and CONNECTED to...

....

....

....

I CELEBRATED...

....

....

....

What challenged me today and how can I shift my thinking tomorrow?

....

....

....

SELF CARE

I took care of myself today by...

....

....

....

I drank ☐ glasses of water today

ON A SCALE OF 1 TO 10, HOW DID I DO TODAY?

THRIVING 10
9
8
7
6
5
4
3
2
1 SURVIVING

Today I am at a ☐

REMEMBER

An hour before I go to bed, I will put my work aside (and my phone), breathe and set my intention for tomorrow.

It's a new day!

TODAY'S
MINDFUL TIP

Get up extra early and
watch the sunrise. As
the sun rises, think of
what this day can bring.

MORNING PRACTICE

My INTENTION for today is...

....

....

....

I am THANKFUL for...

....

....

....

Navigate through the noise and simply FOCUS on
three to-do's:

1 ....

2 ....

3 ....

Welcome today and RELEASE....

....

....

....

AFTERNOON PRACTICE

I LISTENED to...

....

....

....

I RELATED and CONNECTED to...

....

....

....

I CELEBRATED...

....

....

....

What challenged me today and how can I shift my thinking tomorrow?

....

....

....

SELF CARE

I took care of myself today by...

....

....

I drank ☐ glasses of water today

ON A SCALE OF
1 TO 10, HOW DID
I DO TODAY?

THRIVING 10
9
8
7
6
5
4
3
2
1 SURVIVING

Today I am at a ☐

REMEMBER

An hour before I go to bed, I will put my work aside (and my phone), breathe and set my intention for tomorrow.

It's a new day!

TODAY'S MINDFUL TIP

"Be mindful. Be grateful. Be positive. Be true. Be kind."
—Roy T. Bennett

MORNING PRACTICE

My INTENTION for today is...

....

....

....

I am THANKFUL for...

....

....

....

Navigate through the noise and simply FOCUS on three to-do's:

1 ....

2 ....

3 ....

Welcome today and RELEASE....

....

....

....

AFTERNOON PRACTICE

I LISTENED to...

....

....

....

I RELATED and CONNECTED to...

....

....

....

I CELEBRATED...

....

....

....

What challenged me today and how can I shift my thinking tomorrow?

....

....

....

SELF CARE

I took care of myself today by...

....

....

....

I drank ☐ glasses of water today

ON A SCALE OF 1 TO 10, HOW DID I DO TODAY?

↑

THRIVING 10

9

8

7

6

5

4

3

2

1 SURVIVING

Today I am at a ☐

REMEMBER

An hour before I go to bed, I will put my work aside (and my phone), breathe and set my intention for tomorrow.

It's a new day!

TODAY'S MINDFUL TIP

Who inspires you?
Identify a person in your life who lives daily with intention and strives to be the best version of themselves. Appreciate and reflect on the positive influence that person has had in your life and the lives around him or her.

MORNING PRACTICE

My INTENTION for today is...

....

....

....

I am THANKFUL for...

....

....

....

Navigate through the noise and simply FOCUS on three to-do's:

1 ....

2 ....

3 ....

Welcome today and RELEASE....

....

....

....

AFTERNOON PRACTICE

I LISTENED to...

_____

_____

_____

I RELATED and CONNECTED to...

_____

_____

_____

I CELEBRATED...

_____

_____

_____

What challenged me today and how can I shift my thinking tomorrow?

_____

_____

_____

SELF CARE

I took care of myself today by...

_____

_____

I drank ☐ glasses of water today

ON A SCALE OF 1 TO 10, HOW DID I DO TODAY?

THRIVING 10

9

8

7

6

5

4

3

2

1 SURVIVING

Today I am at a ☐

REMEMBER

An hour before I go to bed, I will put my work aside (and my phone), breathe and set my intention for tomorrow.

It's a new day!

TODAY'S MINDFUL TIP

Instead of starting your day with information overload, like checking your email, social media etc..., read an uplifting, inspiring and positive message. Reflect on that message throughout your day.

MORNING PRACTICE

My INTENTION for today is...

....

....

....

I am THANKFUL for...

....

....

....

Navigate through the noise and simply FOCUS on three to-do's:

1 ....

2 ....

3 ....

Welcome today and RELEASE....

....

....

....

AFTERNOON PRACTICE

I LISTENED to...

....

....

....

I RELATED and CONNECTED to...

....

....

....

I CELEBRATED...

....

....

....

What challenged me today and how can I shift my thinking tomorrow?

....

....

....

SELF CARE

I took care of myself today by...

....

....

....

I drank ☐ glasses of water today

ON A SCALE OF
1 TO 10, HOW DID
I DO TODAY?

THRIVING 10
9
8
7
6
5
4
3
2
1 SURVIVING

Today I am at a ☐

REMEMBER

An hour before I go to bed,
I will put my work aside
(and my phone), breathe
and set my intention for
tomorrow.

It's a new day!

TODAY'S MINDFUL TIP

Be grateful for **people**, not just things. People thrive in gratitude. Notice and say thank you. It will do wonders for you and the person receiving it on the other end. A major brain boost.

MORNING PRACTICE

My INTENTION for today is...

....

....

....

I am THANKFUL for...

....

....

....

Navigate through the noise and simply FOCUS on three to-do's:

1 ....

2 ....

3 ....

Welcome today and RELEASE....

....

....

....

AFTERNOON PRACTICE

I LISTENED to...

....

....

....

I RELATED and CONNECTED to...

....

....

....

I CELEBRATED...

....

....

....

What challenged me today and how can I shift my thinking tomorrow?

....

....

....

SELF CARE

I took care of myself today by...

....

....

....

I drank ☐ glasses of water today

ON A SCALE OF 1 TO 10, HOW DID I DO TODAY?

THRIVING 10
9
8
7
6
5
4
3
2
1 SURVIVING

Today I am at a ☐

REMEMBER

An hour before I go to bed, I will put my work aside (and my phone), breathe and set my intention for tomorrow.

It's a new day!

TODAY'S MINDFUL TIP

Drop the judgement in a heated moment with someone. Name it and resist the urge to label it good or bad. Breath through your feelings and be present. Use this in good moments too. This is a tough one!

MORNING PRACTICE

My INTENTION for today is...

....

....

....

I am THANKFUL for...

....

....

....

Navigate through the noise and simply FOCUS on three to-do's:

1 ....

2 ....

3 ....

Welcome today and RELEASE....

....

....

....

AFTERNOON PRACTICE

I LISTENED to...

_____

_____

_____

I RELATED and CONNECTED to...

_____

_____

_____

I CELEBRATED...

_____

_____

_____

What challenged me today and how can I shift my thinking tomorrow?

_____

_____

_____

SELF CARE

I took care of myself today by...

_____

_____

_____

I drank ☐ glasses of water today

ON A SCALE OF 1 TO 10, HOW DID I DO TODAY?

THRIVING ⬆ 10

9

8

7

6

5

4

3

2

1 SURVIVING

Today I am at a ☐

REMEMBER

An hour before I go to bed, I will put my work aside (and my phone), breathe and set my intention for tomorrow.

It's a new day!

TODAY'S MINDFUL TIP

Always Be a Student: It is not about achieving, it's about aspiring to keep getting better. Instead of defaulting to the "can" or "can't" handling of obstacles, we can be curious and open to learn more.

MORNING PRACTICE

My INTENTION for today is...

....

....

....

I am THANKFUL for...

....

....

....

Navigate through the noise and simply FOCUS on three to-do's:

1 ....

2 ....

3 ....

Welcome today and RELEASE....

....

....

....

AFTERNOON PRACTICE

I LISTENED to...

....

....

....

I RELATED and CONNECTED to...

....

....

....

I CELEBRATED...

....

....

....

What challenged me today and how can I shift my thinking tomorrow?

....

....

....

SELF CARE

I took care of myself today by...

....

....

....

I drank [ ] glasses of water today

ON A SCALE OF 1 TO 10, HOW DID I DO TODAY?

THRIVING 10
9
8
7
6
5
4
3
2
1 SURVIVING

Today I am at a [ ]

REMEMBER

An hour before I go to bed, I will put my work aside (and my phone), breathe and set my intention for tomorrow.

It's a new day!

MORNING PRACTICE

My INTENTION for today is...

....

....

....

I am THANKFUL for...

....

....

....

Navigate through the noise and simply FOCUS on three to-do's:

1 ....

2 ....

3 ....

Welcome today and RELEASE....

....

....

....

AFTERNOON PRACTICE

I LISTENED to...

....

....

....

I RELATED and CONNECTED to...

....

....

....

I CELEBRATED...

....

....

....

What challenged me today and how can I shift my thinking tomorrow?

....

....

SELF CARE

I took care of myself today by...

....

....

I drank ☐ glasses of water today

ON A SCALE OF 1 TO 10, HOW DID I DO TODAY?

↑

THRIVING 10

9

8

7

6

5

4

3

2

1 SURVIVING

Today I am at a ☐

REMEMBER

An hour before I go to bed, I will put my work aside (and my phone), breathe and set my intention for tomorrow.

It's a new day!

TODAY'S
MINDFUL TIP

Slow down, sit and watch
the sunset. As the sun
sets; think about what
went well today.

MORNING PRACTICE

My INTENTION for today is...

....
....
....

I am THANKFUL for...

....
....
....

Navigate through the noise and simply FOCUS on
three to-do's:

1 ....

2 ....

3 ....

Welcome today and RELEASE....

....
....
....

AFTERNOON PRACTICE

I LISTENED to...

....

....

....

I RELATED and CONNECTED to...

....

....

....

I CELEBRATED...

....

....

....

What challenged me today and how can I shift my thinking tomorrow?

....

....

....

SELF CARE

I took care of myself today by...

....

....

....

I drank ☐ glasses of water today

ON A SCALE OF 1 TO 10, HOW DID I DO TODAY?

THRIVING   10

9

8

7

6

5

4

3

2

1   SURVIVING

Today I am at a ☐

REMEMBER

An hour before I go to bed, I will put my work aside (and my phone), breathe and set my intention for tomorrow.

DAY 44

It's a new day!

TODAY'S MINDFUL TIP

The tip of the Iceberg:
We all have times where we lose confidence or doubt ourselves. When these feelings rise from beneath the surface, embrace and welcome them without focusing on temporary outcomes. When you touch the truth, it is actually boosting your well-being and confidence.

MORNING PRACTICE

My INTENTION for today is...

....
....
....

I am THANKFUL for...

....
....
....

Navigate through the noise and simply FOCUS on three to-do's:

1 ....

2 ....

3 ....

Welcome today and RELEASE....

....
....
....

AFTERNOON PRACTICE

I LISTENED to...

....

....

....

I RELATED and CONNECTED to...

....

....

....

I CELEBRATED...

....

....

....

What challenged me today and how can I shift my thinking tomorrow?

....

....

....

SELF CARE

I took care of myself today by...

....

....

....

I drank ☐ glasses of water today

ON A SCALE OF I TO 10, HOW DID I DO TODAY?

THRIVING 10

9

8

7

6

5

4

3

2

1 SURVIVING

Today I am at a ☐

REMEMBER

An hour before I go to bed, I will put my work aside (and my phone), breathe and set my intention for tomorrow.

It's a new day!

TODAY'S MINDFUL TIP

Believe and Trust: When faced with a tough choice, it's easy to hand the responsibility over to someone else. Recognize that if you wait for someone else to make decisions for you, you'll waste time and probably not like the decision made anyway! Believe, trust, take charge and hold yourself accountable.

MORNING PRACTICE

My INTENTION for today is...

....

....

....

I am THANKFUL for...

....

....

....

Navigate through the noise and simply FOCUS on three to-do's:

1 ....

2 ....

3 ....

Welcome today and RELEASE....

....

....

....

AFTERNOON PRACTICE

I LISTENED to...

....

....

....

I RELATED and CONNECTED to...

....

....

....

I CELEBRATED...

....

....

....

What challenged me today and how can I shift my thinking tomorrow?

....

....

....

SELF CARE

I took care of myself today by...

....

....

I drank ☐ glasses of water today

ON A SCALE OF 1 TO 10, HOW DID I DO TODAY?

THRIVING 10
9
8
7
6
5
4
3
2
1 SURVIVING

Today I am at a ☐

REMEMBER

An hour before I go to bed, I will put my work aside (and my phone), breathe and set my intention for tomorrow.

It's a new day!

MORNING PRACTICE

My INTENTION for today is...

....

....

....

I am THANKFUL for...

....

....

....

Navigate through the noise and simply FOCUS on three to-do's:

1 ....

2 ....

3 ....

Welcome today and RELEASE....

....

....

....

TODAY'S MINDFUL TIP

Pay attention to detail: Choose a three-minute chunk of your day. Run a mental checklist of your actions. Example: "I am walking toward the school entrance. I am swiping my key. I am opening the door....and so on." In the evening, see how much of those three minutes you can remember compared to any other part of your day.

AFTERNOON PRACTICE

I LISTENED to...

....

....

....

I RELATED and CONNECTED to...

....

....

....

I CELEBRATED...

....

....

....

What challenged me today and how can I shift my thinking tomorrow?

....

....

....

SELF CARE

I took care of myself today by...

....

....

I drank ⬜ glasses of water today

ON A SCALE OF 1 TO 10, HOW DID I DO TODAY?

THRIVING 10
9
8
7
6
5
4
3
2
1 SURVIVING

Today I am at a ⬜

REMEMBER

An hour before I go to bed, I will put my work aside (and my phone), breathe and set my intention for tomorrow.

DAY 47

It's a new day!

MORNING PRACTICE

My INTENTION for today is...

....

....

....

I am THANKFUL for...

....

....

....

Navigate through the noise and simply FOCUS on three to-do's:

1 ....

2 ....

3 ....

Welcome today and RELEASE....

....

....

....

TODAY'S MINDFUL TIP

Are your present?
Answer these three questions: Do you always remember people's names after you have been introduced? Can you remember the last movie you saw and what it was about? Can you recall conversations you had with others this past week? If the answer is no, that's okay. Continue to strengthen your brain to be in the moment.

AFTERNOON PRACTICE

I LISTENED to...

....

....

....

I RELATED and CONNECTED to...

....

....

....

I CELEBRATED...

....

....

....

What challenged me today and how can I shift my thinking tomorrow?

....

....

....

SELF CARE

I took care of myself today by...

....

....

I drank ☐ glasses of water today

ON A SCALE OF 1 TO 10, HOW DID I DO TODAY?

THRIVING 10
9
8
7
6
5
4
3
2
1 SURVIVING

Today I am at a ☐

REMEMBER

An hour before I go to bed, I will put my work aside (and my phone), breathe and set my intention for tomorrow.

DAY 48

It's a new day!

TODAY'S MINDFUL TIP

REFLECT

Reflect on your practices, values and beliefs

Empower yourself and those around you to lead

Find your strengths and the strengths of others around you.

Let go of the NOISE that blocks you from moving forward

Engage in the present moment.

Connect with your colleagues, students and community

Teach what you preach- be authentic.

MORNING PRACTICE

My INTENTION for today is...

....

....

....

I am THANKFUL for...

....

....

....

Navigate through the noise and simply FOCUS on three to-do's:

1 ....

2 ....

3 ....

Welcome today and RELEASE....

....

....

....

AFTERNOON PRACTICE

I LISTENED to...

....

....

....

I RELATED and CONNECTED to...

....

....

....

I CELEBRATED...

....

....

....

What challenged me today and how can I shift my thinking tomorrow?

....

....

....

SELF CARE

I took care of myself today by...

....

....

....

I drank [ ] glasses of water today

ON A SCALE OF 1 TO 10, HOW DID I DO TODAY?

THRIVING 10
9
8
7
6
5
4
3
2
1 SURVIVING

Today I am at a [ ]

REMEMBER

An hour before I go to bed, I will put my work aside (and my phone), breathe and set my intention for tomorrow.

It's a new day!

TODAY'S MINDFUL TIP

Ask and you shall receive. Try asking questions next time someone shares something meaningful with you instead of offering advice or talking about your own experiences with what she/he is going through.

MORNING PRACTICE

My INTENTION for today is...

....

....

....

I am THANKFUL for...

....

....

....

Navigate through the noise and simply FOCUS on three to-do's:

1 ....

2 ....

3 ....

Welcome today and RELEASE....

....

....

....

AFTERNOON PRACTICE

I LISTENED to...

....

....

....

I RELATED and CONNECTED to...

....

....

....

I CELEBRATED...

....

....

....

What challenged me today and how can I shift my thinking tomorrow?

....

....

....

SELF CARE

I took care of myself today by...

....

....

....

I drank ☐ glasses of water today

ON A SCALE OF 1 TO 10, HOW DID I DO TODAY?

THRIVING 10
9
8
7
6
5
4
3
2
1 SURVIVING

Today I am at a ☐

REMEMBER

An hour before I go to bed, I will put my work aside (and my phone), breathe and set my intention for tomorrow.

Resilience Reflection

EMOTIONAL RESILIENCE IS...

a person's ability
to recover after a
setback and to thrive
in the midst
of challenges,
not just survive.

CHECK IN

Reflecting on the last 25 days, how well did I
implement my daily practices (*before school,
after school, self-care, mindfulness*)?

What went WELL?

....

....

....

....

What did I STRUGGLE with?

....

....

....

....

ON ANY GIVEN DAY we experience a myriad of highs and lows. While some emotional resilience comes naturally to us, we all have the ability to increase our capacity over time and thrive.

Look back on the past 25 days. On a scale of 1 to 10, where do I FIND MYSELF on this line? *Add up your daily scores and divide by 25 to indicate your score.* I AM a ☐

1 — 2 — 3 — 4 — 5 — 6 — 7 — 8 — 9 — 10 →

SURVIVING   THRIVING

What ADJUSTMENTS can I make for the next 25 days to THRIVE?

....

....

....

....

....

Keep Going!

You've Got This!

It's a new day!

TODAY'S MINDFUL TIP

The Sound of Music: Taking a break to actively listen to music for a few minutes during your day can help you return to your work in a more positive, peaceful and productive frame of mind. In fact, listening to music can change your brain in ways that improve memory and learning.

MORNING PRACTICE

My INTENTION for today is...

....

....

....

I am THANKFUL for...

....

....

....

Navigate through the noise and simply FOCUS on three to-do's:

1 ....

2 ....

3 ....

Welcome today and RELEASE....

....

....

....

AFTERNOON PRACTICE

I LISTENED to...

....

....

....

I RELATED and CONNECTED to...

....

....

....

I CELEBRATED...

....

....

....

What challenged me today and how can I shift my thinking tomorrow?

....

....

....

SELF CARE

I took care of myself today by...

....

....

....

I drank ☐ glasses of water today

ON A SCALE OF 1 TO 10, HOW DID I DO TODAY?

THRIVING 10

9

8

7

6

5

4

3

2

1 SURVIVING

Today I am at a ☐

REMEMBER

An hour before I go to bed, I will put my work aside (and my phone), breathe and set my intention for tomorrow.

It's a new day!

TODAY'S MINDFUL TIP

Cultivate Humility:
When you are humble, you are grounded in yourself with enough self-assurance and poise that you don't need to show off or act defensive. Working toward humility is a growth experience in which you no longer need to see yourself above others or put yourself below them.

MORNING PRACTICE

My INTENTION for today is...

....
....
....

I am THANKFUL for...

....
....
....

Navigate through the noise and simply FOCUS on three to-do's:

1 ....

2 ....

3 ....

Welcome today and RELEASE....

....
....
....

AFTERNOON PRACTICE

I LISTENED to...

....

....

....

I RELATED and CONNECTED to...

....

....

....

I CELEBRATED...

....

....

....

What challenged me today and how can I shift my thinking tomorrow?

....

....

....

SELF CARE

I took care of myself today by...

....

....

I drank ☐ glasses of water today

ON A SCALE OF 1 TO 10, HOW DID I DO TODAY?

THRIVING 10
9
8
7
6
5
4
3
2
1 SURVIVING

Today I am at a ☐

REMEMBER

An hour before I go to bed, I will put my work aside (and my phone), breathe and set my intention for tomorrow.

It's a new day!

TODAY'S MINDFUL TIP

Notice your body language: Being mindful of how we communicate with others involves your entire body. What you do with your body and your facial expressions communicates to other people your true feelings and intentions more than words do. Our body language doesn't just impact the way others perceive us. It can change the way we feel about ourselves.

MORNING PRACTICE

My INTENTION for today is...

....

....

....

I am THANKFUL for...

....

....

....

Navigate through the noise and simply FOCUS on three to-do's:

1 ....

2 ....

3 ....

Welcome today and RELEASE....

....

....

....

AFTERNOON PRACTICE

I LISTENED to...

....

....

....

I RELATED and CONNECTED to...

....

....

....

I CELEBRATED...

....

....

....

What challenged me today and how can I shift my thinking tomorrow?

....

....

....

SELF CARE

I took care of myself today by...

....

....

....

I drank ☐ glasses of water today

ON A SCALE OF 1 TO 10, HOW DID I DO TODAY?

THRIVING 10

9

8

7

6

5

4

3

2

1 SURVIVING

Today I am at a ☐

REMEMBER

An hour before I go to bed, I will put my work aside (and my phone), breathe and set my intention for tomorrow.

It's a new day!

TODAY'S MINDFUL TIP

Tidy Up! Organizing your clutter is a way to heal, eliminate physical and emotional blocks and move forward. As you face the mess and start cleaning it up, you'll feel better about yourself and have more positive energy.

MORNING PRACTICE

My INTENTION for today is...

....
....
....

I am THANKFUL for...

....
....
....

Navigate through the noise and simply FOCUS on three to-do's:

1 ....

2 ....

3 ....

Welcome today and RELEASE....

....
....
....

AFTERNOON PRACTICE

I LISTENED to...

....

....

....

I RELATED and CONNECTED to...

....

....

....

I CELEBRATED...

....

....

....

What challenged me today and how can I shift my thinking tomorrow?

....

....

SELF CARE

I took care of myself today by...

....

....

I drank ☐ glasses of water today

ON A SCALE OF 1 TO 10, HOW DID I DO TODAY?

THRIVING 10

9

8

7

6

5

4

3

2

1 SURVIVING

Today I am at a ☐

REMEMBER

An hour before I go to bed, I will put my work aside (and my phone), breathe and set my intention for tomorrow.

TODAY'S MINDFUL TIP

"In the end, just three things matter: How well we have lived. How well we have loved. How well we have learned to let go"
—Jack Kornfield

It's a new day!

MORNING PRACTICE

My INTENTION for today is...

....

....

....

I am THANKFUL for...

....

....

....

Navigate through the noise and simply FOCUS on three to-do's:

1 ....

2 ....

3 ....

Welcome today and RELEASE....

....

....

....

AFTERNOON PRACTICE

I LISTENED to...

....

....

....

I RELATED and CONNECTED to...

....

....

....

I CELEBRATED...

....

....

....

What challenged me today and how can I shift my thinking tomorrow?

....

....

....

SELF CARE

I took care of myself today by...

....

....

....

I drank [ ] glasses of water today

ON A SCALE OF 1 TO 10, HOW DID I DO TODAY?

THRIVING 10
9
8
7
6
5
4
3
2
1 SURVIVING

Today I am at a [ ]

REMEMBER

An hour before I go to bed, I will put my work aside (and my phone), breathe and set my intention for tomorrow.

It's a new day!

MORNING PRACTICE

My INTENTION for today is...

....
....
....

I am THANKFUL for...

....
....
....

Navigate through the noise and simply FOCUS on three to-do's:

1 ....

2 ....

3 ....

Welcome today and RELEASE....

....
....
....

AFTERNOON PRACTICE

I LISTENED to...

....

....

....

I RELATED and CONNECTED to...

....

....

....

I CELEBRATED...

....

....

....

What challenged me today and how can I shift my
thinking tomorrow?

....

....

....

SELF CARE

I took care of myself today by...

....

....

I drank ☐ glasses of water today

ON A SCALE OF 1 TO 10, HOW DID I DO TODAY?

THRIVING 10

9

8

7

6

5

4

3

2

1 SURVIVING

Today I am at a ☐

REMEMBER

An hour before I go to bed,
I will put my work aside
(and my phone), breathe
and set my intention for
tomorrow.

DAY 57

It's a new day!

TODAY'S MINDFUL TIP

Just Say No: When we live in the moment, we say yes to the opportunities that present themselves to us and we say no to those that work against our values and goals. This does not mean saying no to people who ask for favors and support. It is an awareness of the noise that distracts us from making room to say yes to the good stuff!

MORNING PRACTICE

My INTENTION for today is...

....

....

....

I am THANKFUL for...

....

....

....

Navigate through the noise and simply FOCUS on three to-do's:

1 ....

2 ....

3 ....

Welcome today and RELEASE....

....

....

....

AFTERNOON PRACTICE

I LISTENED to...

....

....

....

I RELATED and CONNECTED to...

....

....

....

I CELEBRATED...

....

....

....

What challenged me today and how can I shift my thinking tomorrow?

....

....

....

SELF CARE

I took care of myself today by...

....

....

....

I drank ☐ glasses of water today

ON A SCALE OF 1 TO 10, HOW DID I DO TODAY?

THRIVING 10

9

8

7

6

5

4

3

2

1 SURVIVING

Today I am at a ☐

REMEMBER

An hour before I go to bed, I will put my work aside (and my phone), breathe and set my intention for tomorrow.

DAY
58

It's a new day!

TODAY'S MINDFUL TIP

Empathy at its best.
Put yourself inside the mind of someone you are having a conversation with and listen for meaning.

MORNING PRACTICE

My INTENTION for today is...

....
....
....

I am THANKFUL for...

....
....
....

Navigate through the noise and simply FOCUS on three to-do's:

1 ....

2 ....

3 ....

Welcome today and RELEASE....

....
....
....

AFTERNOON PRACTICE

I **LISTENED** to...

....

....

....

I **RELATED** and **CONNECTED** to...

....

....

....

I **CELEBRATED**...

....

....

....

What challenged me today and how can I shift my thinking tomorrow?

....

....

....

SELF CARE

I took care of myself today by...

....

....

I drank ☐ glasses of water today

ON A SCALE OF 1 TO 10, HOW DID I DO TODAY?

THRIVING 10
9
8
7
6
5
4
3
2
1 SURVIVING

Today I am at a ☐

REMEMBER

An hour before I go to bed, I will put my work aside (and my phone), breathe and set my intention for tomorrow.

DAY 59

It's a new day!

TODAY'S MINDFUL TIP

Shut off the autopilot with daily tasks. Unless you fully engage, your mind is likely to wander and your productivity will decline. Try the following: vary the time of day you do repetitive jobs, shuffle the order and look for different ways to do things. An element of change can ignite a positive shift!

MORNING PRACTICE

My INTENTION for today is...

....

....

....

I am THANKFUL for...

....

....

....

Navigate through the noise and simply FOCUS on three to-do's:

1 ....

2 ....

3 ....

Welcome today and RELEASE....

....

....

....

AFTERNOON PRACTICE

I LISTENED to...

....

....

....

I RELATED and CONNECTED to...

....

....

....

I CELEBRATED...

....

....

....

What challenged me today and how can I shift my thinking tomorrow?

....

....

....

SELF CARE

I took care of myself today by...

....

....

I drank ☐ glasses of water today

ON A SCALE OF 1 TO 10, HOW DID I DO TODAY?

THRIVING 10

9

8

7

6

5

4

3

2

1 SURVIVING

Today I am at a ☐

REMEMBER

An hour before I go to bed, I will put my work aside (and my phone), breathe and set my intention for tomorrow.

DAY 60

It's a new day!

TODAY'S MINDFUL TIP

Mindfully end your workday: Instead of **mindlessly** making your way home, take ten minutes to bring your work day to completion so you can free your mind to transition more easily into your evening routine and set yourself up for a more productive and peaceful start to the next day.

MORNING PRACTICE

My INTENTION for today is...

....

....

....

I am THANKFUL for...

....

....

....

Navigate through the noise and simply FOCUS on three to-do's:

1 ....

2 ....

3 ....

Welcome today and RELEASE....

....

....

....

AFTERNOON PRACTICE

I LISTENED to...

....

....

....

I RELATED and CONNECTED to...

....

....

....

I CELEBRATED...

....

....

....

What challenged me today and how can I shift my thinking tomorrow?

....

....

....

SELF CARE

I took care of myself today by...

....

....

....

I drank ☐ glasses of water today

ON A SCALE OF 1 TO 10, HOW DID I DO TODAY?

THRIVING 10
9
8
7
6
5
4
3
2
1 SURVIVING

Today I am at a ☐

REMEMBER

An hour before I go to bed, I will put my work aside (and my phone), breathe and set my intention for tomorrow.

It's a new day!

TODAY'S MINDFUL TIP

"Don't believe everything you think. Thoughts are just that—thoughts."
—Allan Lokos

MORNING PRACTICE

My INTENTION for today is...

....

....

....

I am THANKFUL for...

....

....

....

Navigate through the noise and simply FOCUS on three to-do's:

1 ....

2 ....

3 ....

Welcome today and RELEASE....

....

....

....

AFTERNOON PRACTICE

I LISTENED to...

....

....

....

I RELATED and CONNECTED to...

....

....

....

I CELEBRATED...

....

....

....

What challenged me today and how can I shift my thinking tomorrow?

....

....

....

SELF CARE

I took care of myself today by...

....

....

....

I drank ☐ glasses of water today

ON A SCALE OF 1 TO 10, HOW DID I DO TODAY?

THRIVING 10
9
8
7
6
5
4
3
2
1 SURVIVING

Today I am at a ☐

REMEMBER

An hour before I go to bed, I will put my work aside (and my phone), breathe and set my intention for tomorrow.

It's a new day!

TODAY'S MINDFUL TIP

Be on time. Get into the habit of being on time. You'll save time and energy by letting go of the worry of being late. Build in extra time to start your day feeling more focused and productive. If you end up being early, use the time for yourself!

MORNING PRACTICE

My INTENTION for today is...

....
....
....

I am THANKFUL for...

....
....
....

Navigate through the noise and simply FOCUS on three to-do's:

1 ....

2 ....

3 ....

Welcome today and RELEASE....

....
....
....

AFTERNOON PRACTICE

I LISTENED to...

....

....

....

I RELATED and CONNECTED to...

....

....

....

I CELEBRATED...

....

....

....

What challenged me today and how can I shift my thinking tomorrow?

....

....

....

SELF CARE

I took care of myself today by...

....

....

....

I drank ⬜ glasses of water today

ON A SCALE OF 1 TO 10, HOW DID I DO TODAY?

THRIVING 10

9

8

7

6

5

4

3

2

1 SURVIVING

Today I am at a ⬜

REMEMBER

An hour before I go to bed, I will put my work aside (and my phone), breathe and set my intention for tomorrow.

DAY 63

It's a new day!

TODAY'S MINDFUL TIP

Gimme a Break: We achieve more at the start and end of periods of work or learning than in the middle. Structure your day into disciplined chunks of activity and rest with distinct start and stop times and you'll be more productive. (I use a 30 minute hourglass to remind me).

MORNING PRACTICE

My INTENTION for today is...

....

....

....

I am THANKFUL for...

....

....

....

Navigate through the noise and simply FOCUS on three to-do's:

1 ....

2 ....

3 ....

Welcome today and RELEASE....

....

....

....

AFTERNOON PRACTICE

I LISTENED to...

....

....

....

I RELATED and CONNECTED to...

....

....

....

I CELEBRATED...

....

....

....

What challenged me today and how can I shift my thinking tomorrow?

....

....

....

SELF CARE

I took care of myself today by...

....

....

....

I drank ⬜ glasses of water today

ON A SCALE OF I TO 10, HOW DID I DO TODAY?

THRIVING 10
9
8
7
6
5
4
3
2
1 SURVIVING

Today I am at a ⬜

REMEMBER

An hour before I go to bed, I will put my work aside (and my phone), breathe and set my intention for tomorrow.

DAY 64

It's a new day!

TODAY'S MINDFUL TIP

Notice Kindness: When we notice kindness and other gifts that benefit us, our brains become wired to seek out the positive in any situation. This increases our resiliency. What did you notice today?

MORNING PRACTICE

My **INTENTION** for today is...

....

....

....

I am **THANKFUL** for...

....

....

....

Navigate through the noise and simply **FOCUS** on three to-do's:

1 ....

2 ....

3 ....

Welcome today and **RELEASE**....

....

....

....

AFTERNOON PRACTICE

I LISTENED to...

....

....

....

I RELATED and CONNECTED to...

....

....

....

I CELEBRATED...

....

....

....

What challenged me today and how can I shift my
thinking tomorrow?

....

....

....

SELF CARE

I took care of myself today by...

....

....

....

I drank ☐ glasses of water today

ON A SCALE OF 1 TO 10, HOW DID I DO TODAY?

THRIVING 10
9
8
7
6
5
4
3
2
1 SURVIVING

Today I am at a ☐

REMEMBER

An hour before I go to bed,
I will put my work aside
(and my phone), breathe
and set my intention for
tomorrow.

It's a new day!

TODAY'S MINDFUL TIP

What's love got to do with it? Practice the art of selflessness and put forth the time and effort to unconditionally love someone expecting nothing in return.

MORNING PRACTICE

My INTENTION for today is...

....

....

....

I am THANKFUL for...

....

....

....

Navigate through the noise and simply FOCUS on three to-do's:

1 ....

2 ....

3 ....

Welcome today and RELEASE....

....

....

....

AFTERNOON PRACTICE

I LISTENED to...

_____
_____
_____

I RELATED and CONNECTED to...

_____
_____
_____

I CELEBRATED...

_____
_____
_____

What challenged me today and how can I shift my thinking tomorrow?

_____
_____
_____

SELF CARE

I took care of myself today by...

_____
_____
_____

I drank ☐ glasses of water today

ON A SCALE OF 1 TO 10, HOW DID I DO TODAY?

THRIVING 10
9
8
7
6
5
4
3
2
1 SURVIVING

Today I am at a ☐

REMEMBER

An hour before I go to bed, I will put my work aside (and my phone), breathe and set my intention for tomorrow.

DAY 66

It's a new day!

TODAY'S MINDFUL TIP

Courageous compassion: While it's important to plan and stick to a schedule, always leave room for courageous moments.

MORNING PRACTICE

My INTENTION for today is...

....

....

....

I am THANKFUL for...

....

....

....

Navigate through the noise and simply FOCUS on three to-do's:

1 ....

2 ....

3 ....

Welcome today and RELEASE....

....

....

....

AFTERNOON PRACTICE

I LISTENED to...

....

....

....

I RELATED and CONNECTED to...

....

....

....

I CELEBRATED...

....

....

....

What challenged me today and how can I shift my thinking tomorrow?

....

....

....

SELF CARE

I took care of myself today by...

....

....

I drank ☐ glasses of water today

ON A SCALE OF 1 TO 10, HOW DID I DO TODAY?

THRIVING 10

9

8

7

6

5

4

3

2

1 SURVIVING

Today I am at a ☐

REMEMBER

An hour before I go to bed, I will put my work aside (and my phone), breathe and set my intention for tomorrow.

It's a new day!

TODAY'S MINDFUL TIP

Put the phone down.
Technology distracts us from being present, which discourages connection and compassion. The next time you are eating a meal or in a social setting, turn your phone off. Pay attention. Listen. Make eye contact. Be fully present. Then notice how you feel afterward.

MORNING PRACTICE

My INTENTION for today is...

I am THANKFUL for...

Navigate through the noise and simply FOCUS on three to-do's:

1
2
3

Welcome today and RELEASE....

AFTERNOON PRACTICE

I LISTENED to...

....

....

....

I RELATED and CONNECTED to...

....

....

....

I CELEBRATED...

....

....

....

What challenged me today and how can I shift my thinking tomorrow?

....

....

....

SELF CARE

I took care of myself today by...

....

....

....

I drank ☐ glasses of water today

ON A SCALE OF 1 TO 10, HOW DID I DO TODAY?

THRIVING 10

9

8

7

6

5

4

3

2

1 SURVIVING

Today I am at a ☐

REMEMBER

An hour before I go to bed, I will put my work aside (and my phone), breathe and set my intention for tomorrow.

It's a new day!

TODAY'S MINDFUL TIP

The time is now: Take the initiative to right a wrong with someone important to you at the next possible moment. Don't wait for apologies. Relationships are too precious to throw away.

MORNING PRACTICE

My INTENTION for today is...

....
....
....

I am THANKFUL for...

....
....
....

Navigate through the noise and simply FOCUS on three to-do's:

1 ....

2 ....

3 ....

Welcome today and RELEASE....

....
....
....

AFTERNOON PRACTICE

I LISTENED to...

....

....

....

I RELATED and CONNECTED to...

....

....

....

I CELEBRATED...

....

....

....

What challenged me today and how can I shift my thinking tomorrow?

....

....

....

SELF CARE

I took care of myself today by...

....

....

....

I drank ☐ glasses of water today

ON A SCALE OF
1 TO 10, HOW DID
I DO TODAY?

↑

THRIVING 10

9

8

7

6

5

4

3

2

1 SURVIVING

Today I am at a ☐

REMEMBER

An hour before I go to bed,
I will put my work aside
(and my phone), breathe
and set my intention for
tomorrow.

It's a new day!

MORNING PRACTICE

My INTENTION for today is...

....

....

....

I am THANKFUL for...

....

....

....

Navigate through the noise and simply FOCUS on
three to-do's:

1 ....

2 ....

3 ....

Welcome today and RELEASE....

....

....

....

AFTERNOON PRACTICE

I LISTENED to...

....

....

....

I RELATED and CONNECTED to...

....

....

....

I CELEBRATED...

....

....

....

What challenged me today and how can I shift my thinking tomorrow?

....

....

....

SELF CARE

I took care of myself today by...

....

....

....

I drank ☐ glasses of water today

ON A SCALE OF 1 TO 10, HOW DID I DO TODAY?

THRIVING 10
9
8
7
6
5
4
3
2
1 SURVIVING

Today I am at a ☐

REMEMBER

An hour before I go to bed, I will put my work aside (and my phone), breathe and set my intention for tomorrow.

It's a new day!

MORNING PRACTICE

My **INTENTION** for today is...

....

....

....

I am **THANKFUL** for...

....

....

....

Navigate through the noise and simply **FOCUS** on
three to-do's:

1 ....

2 ....

3 ....

Welcome today and **RELEASE**....

....

....

....

AFTERNOON PRACTICE

I LISTENED to...

....

....

....

I RELATED and CONNECTED to...

....

....

....

I CELEBRATED...

....

....

....

What challenged me today and how can I shift my thinking tomorrow?

....

....

....

SELF CARE

I took care of myself today by...

....

....

I drank ☐ glasses of water today

ON A SCALE OF 1 TO 10, HOW DID I DO TODAY?

THRIVING 10
9
8
7
6
5
4
3
2
1 SURVIVING

Today I am at a ☐

REMEMBER

An hour before I go to bed, I will put my work aside (and my phone), breathe and set my intention for tomorrow.

It's a new day!

TODAY'S MINDFUL TIP

Let's get moving: Just two minutes of exercise is enough to change your mood as long as you raise your heart rate. Anything from marching in place to jumping jacks can supply a surge of neurotransmitters that boost our dopamine and serotonin levels.

MORNING PRACTICE

My INTENTION for today is...

....

....

....

I am THANKFUL for...

....

....

....

Navigate through the noise and simply FOCUS on three to-do's:

1 ....

2 ....

3 ....

Welcome today and RELEASE....

....

....

....

AFTERNOON PRACTICE

I LISTENED to...

....

....

....

I RELATED and CONNECTED to...

....

....

....

I CELEBRATED...

....

....

....

What challenged me today and how can I shift my thinking tomorrow?

....

....

....

SELF CARE

I took care of myself today by...

....

....

....

I drank ☐ glasses of water today

ON A SCALE OF 1 TO 10, HOW DID I DO TODAY?

THRIVING 10
9
8
7
6
5
4
3
2
1 SURVIVING

Today I am at a ☐

REMEMBER

An hour before I go to bed, I will put my work aside (and my phone), breathe and set my intention for tomorrow.

It's a new day!

TODAY'S
MINDFUL TIP

Live with INTENT:
Incubate (pause),
Notice (pay attention),
Trust (your gut),
Express (share and
embrace),
Nurture (be good to
yourself), and
Take action (live it).
—Mallica Chopra

MORNING PRACTICE

My INTENTION for today is...

....
....
....

I am THANKFUL for...

....
....
....

Navigate through the noise and simply FOCUS on three to-do's:

1 ....

2 ....

3 ....

Welcome today and RELEASE....

....
....
....

AFTERNOON PRACTICE

I LISTENED to...

_____

_____

_____

I RELATED and CONNECTED to...

_____

_____

_____

I CELEBRATED...

_____

_____

_____

What challenged me today and how can I shift my thinking tomorrow?

_____

_____

SELF CARE

I took care of myself today by...

_____

_____

I drank ☐ glasses of water today

ON A SCALE OF 1 TO 10, HOW DID I DO TODAY?

THRIVING 10
9
8
7
6
5
4
3
2
1 SURVIVING

Today I am at a ☐

REMEMBER

An hour before I go to bed, I will put my work aside (and my phone), breathe and set my intention for tomorrow.

It's a new day!

MORNING PRACTICE

My INTENTION for today is...

....
....
....

I am THANKFUL for...

....
....
....

Navigate through the noise and simply FOCUS on three to-do's:

1 ....

2 ....

3 ....

Welcome today and RELEASE....

....
....
....

AFTERNOON PRACTICE

I LISTENED to...

....

....

....

I RELATED and CONNECTED to...

....

....

....

I CELEBRATED...

....

....

....

What challenged me today and how can I shift my thinking tomorrow?

....

....

....

SELF CARE

I took care of myself today by...

....

....

....

I drank ☐ glasses of water today

ON A SCALE OF 1 TO 10, HOW DID I DO TODAY?

THRIVING 10

9

8

7

6

5

4

3

2

1 SURVIVING

Today I am at a ☐

REMEMBER

An hour before I go to bed, I will put my work aside (and my phone), breathe and set my intention for tomorrow.

It's a new day!

TODAY'S MINDFUL TIP

Resist no more: It takes courage to see how we resist what makes us uncomfortable. True resolve means feeling restless and uneasy and bringing effort and energy anyway.

MORNING PRACTICE

My INTENTION for today is...

....

....

....

I am THANKFUL for...

....

....

....

Navigate through the noise and simply FOCUS on three to-do's:

1 ....

2 ....

3 ....

Welcome today and RELEASE....

....

....

....

AFTERNOON PRACTICE

I LISTENED to...

....

....

I RELATED and CONNECTED to...

....

....

I CELEBRATED...

....

....

What challenged me today and how can I shift my thinking tomorrow?

....

....

SELF CARE

I took care of myself today by...

....

....

I drank [ ] glasses of water today

ON A SCALE OF 1 TO 10, HOW DID I DO TODAY?

THRIVING 10

9

8

7

6

5

4

3

2

1 SURVIVING

Today I am at a [ ]

REMEMBER

An hour before I go to bed, I will put my work aside (and my phone), breathe and set my intention for tomorrow.

Resilience Reflection

CHECK IN

Reflecting on the last 25 days, how well did I implement my daily practices (*before school, after school, self-care, mindfulness*)?

What went WELL?

....
....
....
....
....

What did I STRUGGLE with?

....
....
....
....

ON ANY GIVEN DAY we experience a myriad of highs and lows. While some emotional resilience comes naturally to us, we all have the ability to increase our capacity over time and thrive.

Look back on the past 25 days. On a scale of 1 to 10, where do I FIND MYSELF on this line? *Add up your daily scores and divide by 25 to indicate your score.* I AM a ☐

1   2   3   4   5   6   7   8   9   10 →

SURVIVING   THRIVING

What ADJUSTMENTS can I make for the next 25 days to THRIVE?

....

....

....

....

Keep Going!

You've Got This!

It's a new day!

MORNING PRACTICE

My INTENTION for today is...

....
....
....

I am THANKFUL for...

....
....
....

Navigate through the noise and simply FOCUS on three to-do's:

1 ....

2 ....

3 ....

Welcome today and RELEASE....

....
....
....

AFTERNOON PRACTICE

I LISTENED to...

....

....

....

I RELATED and CONNECTED to...

....

....

....

I CELEBRATED...

....

....

....

What challenged me today and how can I shift my thinking tomorrow?

....

....

....

SELF CARE

I took care of myself today by...

....

....

....

I drank ☐ glasses of water today

ON A SCALE OF
1 TO 10, HOW DID
I DO TODAY?

THRIVING 10
9
8
7
6
5
4
3
2
1 SURVIVING

Today I am at a ☐

REMEMBER

An hour before I go to bed, I will put my work aside (and my phone), breathe and set my intention for tomorrow.

It's a new day!

Open up. Be open to different viewpoints and shift your thinking if necessary. It is called wisdom not weakness.

MORNING PRACTICE

My INTENTION for today is...

....
....
....

I am THANKFUL for...

....
....
....

Navigate through the noise and simply FOCUS on three to-do's:

1 ....

2 ....

3 ....

Welcome today and RELEASE....

....
....
....

AFTERNOON PRACTICE

I **LISTENED** to...

....

....

....

I **RELATED** and **CONNECTED** to...

....

....

....

I **CELEBRATED**...

....

....

....

What challenged me today and how can I shift my thinking tomorrow?

....

....

....

SELF CARE

I took care of myself today by...

....

....

....

I drank ☐ glasses of water today

ON A SCALE OF
1 TO 10, HOW DID
I DO TODAY?

THRIVING 10
9
8
7
6
5
4
3
2
1 SURVIVING

Today I am at a ☐

REMEMBER

An hour before I go to bed, I will put my work aside (and my phone), breathe and set my intention for tomorrow.

It's a new day!

MORNING PRACTICE

My INTENTION for today is...

....

....

....

I am THANKFUL for...

....

....

....

Navigate through the noise and simply FOCUS on three to-do's:

1 ....

2 ....

3 ....

Welcome today and RELEASE....

....

....

....

AFTERNOON PRACTICE

I LISTENED to...

....

....

....

I RELATED and CONNECTED to...

....

....

....

I CELEBRATED...

....

....

....

What challenged me today and how can I shift my thinking tomorrow?

....

....

....

SELF CARE

I took care of myself today by...

....

....

....

I drank ☐ glasses of water today

ON A SCALE OF 1 TO 10, HOW DID I DO TODAY?

THRIVING 10

9

8

7

6

5

4

3

2

1 SURVIVING

Today I am at a ☐

REMEMBER

An hour before I go to bed, I will put my work aside (and my phone), breathe and set my intention for tomorrow.

DAY 79

It's a new day!

TODAY'S MINDFUL TIP

Find your purpose: What do I care about beyond myself? What small action can I take that is in line with this belief? Do that one small action today.

MORNING PRACTICE

My INTENTION for today is...

....

....

....

I am THANKFUL for...

....

....

....

Navigate through the noise and simply FOCUS on three to-do's:

1 ....

2 ....

3 ....

Welcome today and RELEASE....

....

....

....

AFTERNOON PRACTICE

I LISTENED to...

....

....

....

I RELATED and CONNECTED to...

....

....

....

I CELEBRATED...

....

....

....

What challenged me today and how can I shift my thinking tomorrow?

....

....

....

SELF CARE

I took care of myself today by...

....

....

....

I drank ☐ glasses of water today

ON A SCALE OF 1 TO 10, HOW DID I DO TODAY?

↑

THRIVING 10

9

8

7

6

5

4

3

2

1 SURVIVING

Today I am at a ☐

REMEMBER

An hour before I go to bed, I will put my work aside (and my phone), breathe and set my intention for tomorrow.

It's a new day!

TODAY'S MINDFUL TIP

Dip and dodge! Every time you are faced with negativity, deflect it with positivity. After a few times, it will become a habit.

MORNING PRACTICE

My INTENTION for today is...

....
....
....

I am THANKFUL for...

....
....
....

Navigate through the noise and simply FOCUS on three to-do's:

1 ....

2 ....

3 ....

Welcome today and RELEASE....

....
....
....

AFTERNOON PRACTICE

I LISTENED to...

....

....

....

I RELATED and CONNECTED to...

....

....

....

I CELEBRATED...

....

....

....

What challenged me today and how can I shift my thinking tomorrow?

....

....

....

SELF CARE

I took care of myself today by...

....

....

....

I drank ☐ glasses of water today

ON A SCALE OF 1 TO 10, HOW DID I DO TODAY?

THRIVING 10
9
8
7
6
5
4
3
2
1 SURVIVING

Today I am at a ☐

REMEMBER

An hour before I go to bed, I will put my work aside (and my phone), breathe and set my intention for tomorrow.

It's a new day!

TODAY'S MINDFUL TIP

Take a minute to sit and look at the immediate area and see if you notice things that you have not noticed before. It is incredible when we realize there has been something right in front of us but we just did not take the time to notice.

MORNING PRACTICE

My INTENTION for today is...

....

....

....

I am THANKFUL for...

....

....

....

Navigate through the noise and simply FOCUS on three to-do's:

1 ....

2 ....

3 ....

Welcome today and RELEASE....

....

....

....

AFTERNOON PRACTICE

I LISTENED to...

....

....

....

I RELATED and CONNECTED to...

....

....

....

I CELEBRATED...

....

....

....

What challenged me today and how can I shift my thinking tomorrow?

....

....

....

SELF CARE

I took care of myself today by...

....

....

I drank ☐ glasses of water today

ON A SCALE OF 1 TO 10, HOW DID I DO TODAY?

THRIVING 10

9

8

7

6

5

4

3

2

1 SURVIVING

Today I am at a ☐

REMEMBER

An hour before I go to bed, I will put my work aside (and my phone), breathe and set my intention for tomorrow.

It's a new day!

TODAY'S MINDFUL TIP

Change it up. Today do something different. Getting out of the daily routine ignites energy.

MORNING PRACTICE

My INTENTION for today is...

....
....
....

I am THANKFUL for...

....
....
....

Navigate through the noise and simply FOCUS on three to-do's:

1 ....

2 ....

3 ....

Welcome today and RELEASE....

....
....
....

AFTERNOON PRACTICE

I LISTENED to...

....

....

....

I RELATED and CONNECTED to...

....

....

....

I CELEBRATED...

....

....

....

What challenged me today and how can I shift my
thinking tomorrow?

....

....

....

SELF CARE

I took care of myself today by...

....

....

I drank [ ] glasses of water today

ON A SCALE OF 1 TO 10, HOW DID I DO TODAY?

THRIVING 10

9

8

7

6

5

4

3

2

1 SURVIVING

Today I am at a [ ]

REMEMBER

An hour before I go to bed,
I will put my work aside
(and my phone), breathe
and set my intention for
tomorrow.

It's a new day!

TODAY'S MINDFUL TIP

Spread kindness.
Next time you are sitting down with a group of people, ask for each person to give a compliment to the person next to them. Then reverse, so each person gives and receives two compliments.

MORNING PRACTICE

My INTENTION for today is...

....

....

....

I am THANKFUL for...

....

....

....

Navigate through the noise and simply FOCUS on three to-do's:

1 ....

2 ....

3 ....

Welcome today and RELEASE....

....

....

....

AFTERNOON PRACTICE

I LISTENED to...

_____

_____

_____

I RELATED and CONNECTED to...

_____

_____

_____

I CELEBRATED...

_____

_____

_____

What challenged me today and how can I shift my thinking tomorrow?

_____

_____

_____

SELF CARE

I took care of myself today by...

_____

_____

I drank ☐ glasses of water today

ON A SCALE OF 1 TO 10, HOW DID I DO TODAY?

THRIVING 10

9

8

7

6

5

4

3

2

1 SURVIVING

Today I am at a ☐

REMEMBER

An hour before I go to bed, I will put my work aside (and my phone), breathe and set my intention for tomorrow.

It's a new day!

Ask permission to offer your two cents. When you ask to open the door, as opposed to barging in, there is a better chance of it staying open.

MORNING PRACTICE

My INTENTION for today is...

....

....

....

I am THANKFUL for...

....

....

....

Navigate through the noise and simply FOCUS on three to-do's:

1 ....

2 ....

3 ....

Welcome today and RELEASE....

....

....

....

AFTERNOON PRACTICE

I LISTENED to...

....

....

....

I RELATED and CONNECTED to...

....

....

....

I CELEBRATED...

....

....

....

What challenged me today and how can I shift my thinking tomorrow?

....

....

....

SELF CARE

I took care of myself today by...

....

....

....

I drank ☐ glasses of water today

ON A SCALE OF 1 TO 10, HOW DID I DO TODAY?

THRIVING 10

9

8

7

6

5

4

3

2

1 SURVIVING

Today I am at a ☐

REMEMBER

An hour before I go to bed, I will put my work aside (and my phone), breathe and set my intention for tomorrow.

It's a new day!

TODAY'S
MINDFUL TIP

"Sometimes you need to
sit lonely on the floor in
a quiet room in order to
hear your own voice and
not let it drown in the
noise of others."
—Charlotte Eriksson

MORNING PRACTICE

My INTENTION for today is...

....
....
....

I am THANKFUL for...

....
....
....

Navigate through the noise and simply FOCUS on
three to-do's:

1 ....

2 ....

3 ....

Welcome today and RELEASE....

....
....
....

AFTERNOON PRACTICE

I LISTENED to...

....

....

....

I RELATED and CONNECTED to...

....

....

....

I CELEBRATED...

....

....

....

What challenged me today and how can I shift my thinking tomorrow?

....

....

....

SELF CARE

I took care of myself today by...

....

....

....

I drank ☐ glasses of water today

ON A SCALE OF 1 TO 10, HOW DID I DO TODAY?

↑

THRIVING 10

9

8

7

6

5

4

3

2

1 SURVIVING

Today I am at a ☐

REMEMBER

An hour before I go to bed, I will put my work aside (and my phone), breathe and set my intention for tomorrow.

It's a new day!

TODAY'S MINDFUL TIP

Visit with a colleague you usually don't spend time with.

MORNING PRACTICE

My INTENTION for today is...

....

....

....

I am THANKFUL for...

....

....

....

Navigate through the noise and simply FOCUS on three to-do's:

1 ....

2 ....

3 ....

Welcome today and RELEASE....

....

....

....

AFTERNOON PRACTICE

I LISTENED to...

....

....

....

I RELATED and CONNECTED to...

....

....

....

I CELEBRATED...

....

....

....

What challenged me today and how can I shift my thinking tomorrow?

....

....

....

SELF CARE

I took care of myself today by...

....

....

I drank ☐ glasses of water today

ON A SCALE OF 1 TO 10, HOW DID I DO TODAY?

THRIVING 10

9

8

7

6

5

4

3

2

1   SURVIVING

Today I am at a ☐

REMEMBER

An hour before I go to bed, I will put my work aside (and my phone), breathe and set my intention for tomorrow.

It's a new day!

TODAY'S
MINDFUL TIP

Diffuse a situation
by coming up with a
solution rather than
focusing on the problem.

MORNING PRACTICE

My INTENTION for today is...

....
....
....

I am THANKFUL for...

....
....
....

Navigate through the noise and simply FOCUS on three to-do's:

1 ....

2 ....

3 ....

Welcome today and RELEASE....

....
....
....

AFTERNOON PRACTICE

I LISTENED to...

....

....

....

I RELATED and CONNECTED to...

....

....

....

I CELEBRATED...

....

....

....

What challenged me today and how can I shift my thinking tomorrow?

....

....

....

SELF CARE

I took care of myself today by...

....

....

I drank ☐ glasses of water today

ON A SCALE OF 1 TO 10, HOW DID I DO TODAY?

THRIVING 10
9
8
7
6
5
4
3
2
1 SURVIVING

Today I am at a ☐

REMEMBER

An hour before I go to bed, I will put my work aside (and my phone), breathe and set my intention for tomorrow.

DAY 88

It's a new day!

TODAY'S MINDFUL TIP

Say **thank you** to someone who has a made a difference in your day.

MORNING PRACTICE

My INTENTION for today is...

....

....

....

I am THANKFUL for...

....

....

....

Navigate through the noise and simply FOCUS on three to-do's:

1 ....

2 ....

3 ....

Welcome today and RELEASE....

....

....

....

AFTERNOON PRACTICE

I LISTENED to...

....

....

....

I RELATED and CONNECTED to...

....

....

....

I CELEBRATED...

....

....

....

What challenged me today and how can I shift my thinking tomorrow?

....

....

....

SELF CARE

I took care of myself today by...

....

....

I drank ☐ glasses of water today

ON A SCALE OF 1 TO 10, HOW DID I DO TODAY?

THRIVING 10
9
8
7
6
5
4
3
2
1 SURVIVING

Today I am at a ☐

REMEMBER

An hour before I go to bed, I will put my work aside (and my phone), breathe and set my intention for tomorrow.

It's a new day!

MORNING PRACTICE

My INTENTION for today is...

....

....

....

I am THANKFUL for...

....

....

....

Navigate through the noise and simply FOCUS on three to-do's:

1 ....

2 ....

3 ....

Welcome today and RELEASE....

....

....

....

AFTERNOON PRACTICE

I LISTENED to...

....

....

....

I RELATED and CONNECTED to...

....

....

....

I CELEBRATED...

....

....

....

What challenged me today and how can I shift my thinking tomorrow?

....

....

....

SELF CARE

I took care of myself today by...

....

....

....

I drank [ ] glasses of water today

ON A SCALE OF 1 TO 10, HOW DID I DO TODAY?

THRIVING 10
9
8
7
6
5
4
3
2
1 SURVIVING

Today I am at a [ ]

REMEMBER

An hour before I go to bed, I will put my work aside (and my phone), breathe and set my intention for tomorrow.

It's a new day!

TODAY'S MINDFUL TIP

It's brinner time! Have breakfast for dinner. So often, we rush to eat something in the morning. Why not enjoy it when you are not pressed for time? Make a nice healthy portion of your favorite breakfast foods and end the day with a meal you love!

MORNING PRACTICE

My INTENTION for today is...

....

....

....

I am THANKFUL for...

....

....

....

Navigate through the noise and simply FOCUS on three to-do's:

1 ....

2 ....

3 ....

Welcome today and RELEASE....

....

....

....

AFTERNOON PRACTICE

I LISTENED to...

....

....

....

I RELATED and CONNECTED to...

....

....

....

I CELEBRATED...

....

....

....

What challenged me today and how can I shift my thinking tomorrow?

....

....

....

SELF CARE

I took care of myself today by...

....

....

....

I drank ☐ glasses of water today

ON A SCALE OF 1 TO 10, HOW DID I DO TODAY?

THRIVING 10
9
8
7
6
5
4
3
2
1 SURVIVING

Today I am at a ☐

REMEMBER

An hour before I go to bed, I will put my work aside (and my phone), breathe and set my intention for tomorrow.

It's a new day!

TODAY'S MINDFUL TIP

"Your mind is a flexible mirror, adjust it, to see a better world."
—Amit Ray

MORNING PRACTICE

My INTENTION for today is...

....

....

....

I am THANKFUL for...

....

....

....

Navigate through the noise and simply FOCUS on three to-do's:

1 ....

2 ....

3 ....

Welcome today and RELEASE....

....

....

....

AFTERNOON PRACTICE

I LISTENED to...

....

....

....

I RELATED and CONNECTED to...

....

....

....

I CELEBRATED...

....

....

....

What challenged me today and how can I shift my thinking tomorrow?

....

....

....

SELF CARE

I took care of myself today by...

....

....

....

I drank ☐ glasses of water today

ON A SCALE OF
I TO 10, HOW DID
I DO TODAY?

THRIVING 10

9

8

7

6

5

4

3

2

1   SURVIVING

Today I am at a ☐

REMEMBER

An hour before I go to bed,
I will put my work aside
(and my phone), breathe
and set my intention for
tomorrow.

It's a new day!

MORNING PRACTICE

My INTENTION for today is...

....

....

....

I am THANKFUL for...

....

....

....

Navigate through the noise and simply FOCUS on three to-do's:

1 ....

2 ....

3 ....

Welcome today and RELEASE....

....

....

....

AFTERNOON PRACTICE

I LISTENED to...

....
....
....

I RELATED and CONNECTED to...

....
....
....

I CELEBRATED...

....
....
....

What challenged me today and how can I shift my thinking tomorrow?

....
....

SELF CARE

I took care of myself today by...

....
....
....

I drank ☐ glasses of water today

ON A SCALE OF 1 TO 10, HOW DID I DO TODAY?

THRIVING 10
9
8
7
6
5
4
3
2
1 SURVIVING

Today I am at a ☐

REMEMBER

An hour before I go to bed, I will put my work aside (and my phone), breathe and set my intention for tomorrow.

It's a new day!

MORNING PRACTICE

My INTENTION for today is...

....

....

....

I am THANKFUL for...

....

....

....

Navigate through the noise and simply FOCUS on three to-do's:

1 ....

2 ....

3 ....

Welcome today and RELEASE....

....

....

....

AFTERNOON PRACTICE

I LISTENED to...

....

....

....

I RELATED and CONNECTED to...

....

....

....

I CELEBRATED...

....

....

....

What challenged me today and how can I shift my thinking tomorrow?

....

....

....

SELF CARE

I took care of myself today by...

....

....

....

I drank ☐ glasses of water today

ON A SCALE OF 1 TO 10, HOW DID I DO TODAY?

THRIVING 10

9

8

7

6

5

4

3

2

1 SURVIVING

Today I am at a ☐

REMEMBER

An hour before I go to bed, I will put my work aside (and my phone), breathe and set my intention for tomorrow.

It's a new day!

MORNING PRACTICE

My INTENTION for today is...

....

....

....

I am THANKFUL for...

....

....

....

Navigate through the noise and simply FOCUS on three to-do's:

1 ....

2 ....

3 ....

Welcome today and RELEASE....

....

....

....

AFTERNOON PRACTICE

I LISTENED to...

....

....

....

I RELATED and CONNECTED to...

....

....

....

I CELEBRATED...

....

....

....

What challenged me today and how can I shift my thinking tomorrow?

....

....

....

SELF CARE

I took care of myself today by...

....

....

....

I drank ☐ glasses of water today

ON A SCALE OF 1 TO 10, HOW DID I DO TODAY?

↑

THRIVING 10

9

8

7

6

5

4

3

2

1 SURVIVING

Today I am at a ☐

REMEMBER

An hour before I go to bed, I will put my work aside (and my phone), breathe and set my intention for tomorrow.

DAY 95

It's a new day!

MORNING PRACTICE

My INTENTION for today is...

....

....

....

I am THANKFUL for...

....

....

....

Navigate through the noise and simply FOCUS on three to-do's:

1 ....

2 ....

3 ....

Welcome today and RELEASE....

....

....

....

AFTERNOON PRACTICE

I LISTENED to...

....
....
....

I RELATED and CONNECTED to...

....
....
....

I CELEBRATED...

....
....
....

What challenged me today and how can I shift my thinking tomorrow?

....
....
....

SELF CARE

I took care of myself today by...

....
....
....

I drank ☐ glasses of water today

ON A SCALE OF 1 TO 10, HOW DID I DO TODAY?

THRIVING 10
9
8
7
6
5
4
3
2
1 SURVIVING

Today I am at a ☐

REMEMBER

An hour before I go to bed, I will put my work aside (and my phone), breathe and set my intention for tomorrow.

It's a new day!

MORNING PRACTICE

My INTENTION for today is...

....
....
....

I am THANKFUL for...

....
....
....

Navigate through the noise and simply FOCUS on three to-do's:

1 ....

2 ....

3 ....

Welcome today and RELEASE....

....
....
....

TODAY'S MINDFUL TIP

Do a top 10 list of things and people in your life that bring you joy.

AFTERNOON PRACTICE

I LISTENED to...

....

....

....

I RELATED and CONNECTED to...

....

....

....

I CELEBRATED...

....

....

....

What challenged me today and how can I shift my thinking tomorrow?

....

....

....

SELF CARE

I took care of myself today by...

....

....

I drank [ ] glasses of water today

ON A SCALE OF I TO 10, HOW DID I DO TODAY?

THRIVING 10
9
8
7
6
5
4
3
2
I SURVIVING

Today I am at a [ ]

REMEMBER

An hour before I go to bed, I will put my work aside (and my phone), breathe and set my intention for tomorrow.

It's a new day!

MORNING PRACTICE

My INTENTION for today is...

....

....

....

I am THANKFUL for...

....

....

....

Navigate through the noise and simply FOCUS on three to-do's:

1 ....

2 ....

3 ....

Welcome today and RELEASE....

....

....

....

AFTERNOON PRACTICE

I LISTENED to...

....

....

....

I RELATED and CONNECTED to...

....

....

....

I CELEBRATED...

....

....

....

What challenged me today and how can I shift my thinking tomorrow?

....

....

....

SELF CARE

I took care of myself today by...

....

....

....

I drank ☐ glasses of water today

ON A SCALE OF 1 TO 10, HOW DID I DO TODAY?

↑

THRIVING 10

9

8

7

6

5

4

3

2

1 SURVIVING

Today I am at a ☐

REMEMBER

An hour before I go to bed, I will put my work aside (and my phone), breathe and set my intention for tomorrow.

It's a new day!

TODAY'S MINDFUL TIP

"Respond; don't react.
Listen; don't talk.
Think; don't assume."
—Raji Lukkoor

MORNING PRACTICE

My INTENTION for today is...

....

....

....

I am THANKFUL for...

....

....

....

Navigate through the noise and simply FOCUS on three to-do's:

1 ....

2 ....

3 ....

Welcome today and RELEASE....

....

....

....

AFTERNOON PRACTICE

I LISTENED to...

....

....

....

I RELATED and CONNECTED to...

....

....

....

I CELEBRATED...

....

....

....

What challenged me today and how can I shift my thinking tomorrow?

....

....

....

SELF CARE

I took care of myself today by...

....

....

....

I drank ☐ glasses of water today

ON A SCALE OF 1 TO 10, HOW DID I DO TODAY?

THRIVING 10

9

8

7

6

5

4

3

2

1 SURVIVING

Today I am at a ☐

REMEMBER

An hour before I go to bed, I will put my work aside (and my phone), breathe and set my intention for tomorrow.

It's a new day!

MORNING PRACTICE

My INTENTION for today is...

....
....
....

I am THANKFUL for...

....
....
....

Navigate through the noise and simply FOCUS on three to-do's:

1 ....

2 ....

3 ....

Welcome today and RELEASE....

....
....
....

AFTERNOON PRACTICE

I LISTENED to...

....

....

....

I RELATED and CONNECTED to...

....

....

....

I CELEBRATED...

....

....

....

What challenged me today and how can I shift my thinking tomorrow?

....

....

....

SELF CARE

I took care of myself today by...

....

....

....

I drank ☐ glasses of water today

ON A SCALE OF 1 TO 10, HOW DID I DO TODAY?

THRIVING 10

9

8

7

6

5

4

3

2

1 SURVIVING

Today I am at a ☐

REMEMBER

An hour before I go to bed, I will put my work aside (and my phone), breathe and set my intention for tomorrow.

Resilience Reflection

EMOTIONAL
RESILIENCE
IS...

a person's ability
to recover after a
setback and to thrive
in the midst
of challenges,
not just survive.

CHECK IN

Reflecting on the last 25 days, how well did I
implement my daily practices (*before school,
after school, self-care, mindfulness*)?

What went WELL?

....
....
....
....

What did I STRUGGLE with?

....
....
....
....

ON ANY GIVEN DAY we experience a myriad of highs and lows. While some emotional resilience comes naturally to us, we all have the ability to increase our capacity over time and thrive.

Look back on the past 25 days. On a scale of 1 to 10, where do I **FIND MYSELF** on this line? *Add up your daily scores and divide by 25 to indicate your score.* I AM a ☐

1   2   3   4   5   6   7   8   9   10 →

SURVIVING   THRIVING

What **ADJUSTMENTS** can I make for the next 25 days to **THRIVE**?

....

....

....

....

Keep Going!
You've Got This!

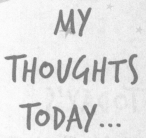

_____

_____

_____

_____

_____

_____

_____

_____

_____

_____

_____

_____

_____

It's a new day!

MORNING PRACTICE

My INTENTION for today is...

....

....

....

I am THANKFUL for...

....

....

....

Navigate through the noise and simply FOCUS on three to-do's:

1 ....

2 ....

3 ....

Welcome today and RELEASE....

....

....

....

TODAY'S MINDFUL TIP

"Hold yourself responsible for a higher standard than anyone else expects of you. Never excuse yourself."
—Henry Ward Beecher

AFTERNOON PRACTICE

I LISTENED to...

....

....

....

I RELATED and CONNECTED to...

....

....

....

I CELEBRATED...

....

....

....

What challenged me today and how can I shift my thinking tomorrow?

....

....

....

SELF CARE

I took care of myself today by...

....

....

I drank ⬜ glasses of water today

ON A SCALE OF 1 TO 10, HOW DID I DO TODAY?

↑

THRIVING   10

9

8

7

6

5

4

3

2

1   SURVIVING

Today I am at a ⬜

REMEMBER

An hour before I go to bed, I will put my work aside (and my phone), breathe and set my intention for tomorrow.

It's a new day!

TODAY'S MINDFUL TIP

Show your mind who's boss! To be in charge is not about controlling your mind, it's about seeing your thoughts for what they are. Take time today to look at your thoughts and TRUST that you can handle whatever happens and that things will work out.

MORNING PRACTICE

My INTENTION for today is...

....

....

....

I am THANKFUL for...

....

....

....

Navigate through the noise and simply FOCUS on three to-do's:

1 ....

2 ....

3 ....

Welcome today and RELEASE....

....

....

....

AFTERNOON PRACTICE

I LISTENED to...

_____

_____

_____

I RELATED and CONNECTED to...

_____

_____

_____

I CELEBRATED...

_____

_____

_____

What challenged me today and how can I shift my thinking tomorrow?

_____

_____

_____

SELF CARE

I took care of myself today by...

_____

_____

_____

I drank ☐ glasses of water today

ON A SCALE OF 1 TO 10, HOW DID I DO TODAY?

THRIVING 10
9
8
7
6
5
4
3
2
1 SURVIVING

Today I am at a ☐

REMEMBER

An hour before I go to bed, I will put my work aside (and my phone), breathe and set my intention for tomorrow.

It's a new day!

TODAY'S MINDFUL TIP

For every negative thought that enters your mind, replace it with two positive thoughts. This includes thoughts about yourself and/or others!

MORNING PRACTICE

My INTENTION for today is...

....

....

....

I am THANKFUL for...

....

....

....

Navigate through the noise and simply FOCUS on three to-do's:

1 ....

2 ....

3 ....

Welcome today and RELEASE....

....

....

....

AFTERNOON PRACTICE

I LISTENED to...

_____

_____

_____

I RELATED and CONNECTED to...

_____

_____

_____

I CELEBRATED...

_____

_____

_____

What challenged me today and how can I shift my thinking tomorrow?

_____

_____

_____

SELF CARE

I took care of myself today by...

_____

_____

_____

I drank [　] glasses of water today

ON A SCALE OF 1 TO 10, HOW DID I DO TODAY?

THRIVING 10
9
8
7
6
5
4
3
2
1 SURVIVING

Today I am at a [　]

REMEMBER

An hour before I go to bed, I will put my work aside (and my phone), breathe and set my intention for tomorrow.

It's a new day!

TODAY'S MINDFUL TIP

"Mindful eating is about awareness. When you eat mindfully, you slow down, pay attention to the food you're eating and savor every bite."
—Susan Albers

MORNING PRACTICE

My INTENTION for today is...

....

....

....

I am THANKFUL for...

....

....

....

Navigate through the noise and simply FOCUS on three to-do's:

1 ....

2 ....

3 ....

Welcome today and RELEASE....

....

....

....

AFTERNOON PRACTICE

I LISTENED to...

....

....

....

I RELATED and CONNECTED to...

....

....

....

I CELEBRATED...

....

....

....

What challenged me today and how can I shift my thinking tomorrow?

....

....

....

SELF CARE

I took care of myself today by...

....

....

....

I drank ☐ glasses of water today

ON A SCALE OF 1 TO 10, HOW DID I DO TODAY?

THRIVING 10

9

8

7

6

5

4

3

2

1 SURVIVING

Today I am at a ☐

REMEMBER

An hour before I go to bed, I will put my work aside (and my phone), breathe and set my intention for tomorrow.

It's a new day!

MORNING PRACTICE

My INTENTION for today is...

....

....

....

I am THANKFUL for...

....

....

....

Navigate through the noise and simply FOCUS on three to-do's:

1 ....

2 ....

3 ....

Welcome today and RELEASE....

....

....

....

AFTERNOON PRACTICE

I LISTENED to...

....

....

....

I RELATED and CONNECTED to...

....

....

....

I CELEBRATED...

....

....

....

What challenged me today and how can I shift my thinking tomorrow?

....

....

....

SELF CARE

I took care of myself today by...

....

....

....

I drank ☐ glasses of water today

ON A SCALE OF 1 TO 10, HOW DID I DO TODAY?

THRIVING 10
9
8
7
6
5
4
3
2
1 SURVIVING

Today I am at a ☐

REMEMBER

An hour before I go to bed, I will put my work aside (and my phone), breathe and set my intention for tomorrow.

It's a new day!

TODAY'S MINDFUL TIP

Relax by closing your eyes, taking three deep breaths and counting backward from 20. Feel the rhythm of your chest and diaphragm rising and falling with each number.

MORNING PRACTICE

My INTENTION for today is...

....

....

....

I am THANKFUL for...

....

....

....

Navigate through the noise and simply FOCUS on three to-do's:

1 ....

2 ....

3 ....

Welcome today and RELEASE....

....

....

....

AFTERNOON PRACTICE

I LISTENED to...

....

....

....

I RELATED and CONNECTED to...

....

....

....

I CELEBRATED...

....

....

....

What challenged me today and how can I shift my thinking tomorrow?

....

....

....

SELF CARE

I took care of myself today by...

....

....

....

I drank ☐ glasses of water today

ON A SCALE OF 1 TO 10, HOW DID I DO TODAY?

THRIVING 10
9
8
7
6
5
4
3
2
1 SURVIVING

Today I am at a ☐

REMEMBER

An hour before I go to bed, I will put my work aside (and my phone), breathe and set my intention for tomorrow.

It's a new day!

TODAY'S
MINDFUL TIP

Are you a natural
talker or do you prefer
listening? Do what does
NOT come naturally
to you today. Minimize
talking while maximizing
listening or flip it to
maximize talking and
minimize listening and
see what you learn today
about yourself and
others.

MORNING PRACTICE

My INTENTION for today is...

....

....

....

I am THANKFUL for...

....

....

....

Navigate through the noise and simply FOCUS on three to-do's:

1 ....

2 ....

3 ....

Welcome today and RELEASE....

....

....

....

AFTERNOON PRACTICE

I LISTENED to...

....

....

....

I RELATED and CONNECTED to...

....

....

....

I CELEBRATED...

....

....

....

What challenged me today and how can I shift my thinking tomorrow?

....

....

....

SELF CARE

I took care of myself today by...

....

....

....

I drank ☐ glasses of water today

ON A SCALE OF 1 TO 10, HOW DID I DO TODAY?

THRIVING 10
9
8
7
6
5
4
3
2
1 SURVIVING

Today I am at a ☐

REMEMBER

An hour before I go to bed, I will put my work aside (and my phone), breathe and set my intention for tomorrow.

It's a new day!

TODAY'S MINDFUL TIP

Simplify. Less is more. When we exhale and simplify our daily life, fewer decisions have to made and more time is available in the day.

MORNING PRACTICE

My INTENTION for today is...

....
....
....

I am THANKFUL for...

....
....
....

Navigate through the noise and simply FOCUS on three to-do's:

1 ....

2 ....

3 ....

Welcome today and RELEASE....

....
....
....

AFTERNOON PRACTICE

I LISTENED to...

....

....

....

I RELATED and CONNECTED to...

....

....

....

I CELEBRATED...

....

....

....

What challenged me today and how can I shift my thinking tomorrow?

....

....

....

SELF CARE

I took care of myself today by...

....

....

....

I drank ☐ glasses of water today

ON A SCALE OF 1 TO 10, HOW DID I DO TODAY?

THRIVING 10
9
8
7
6
5
4
3
2
1 SURVIVING

Today I am at a ☐

REMEMBER

An hour before I go to bed, I will put my work aside (and my phone), breathe and set my intention for tomorrow.

It's a new day!

MORNING PRACTICE

My INTENTION for today is...

....

....

....

I am THANKFUL for...

....

....

....

Navigate through the noise and simply FOCUS on three to-do's:

1 ....

2 ....

3 ....

Welcome today and RELEASE....

....

....

....

AFTERNOON PRACTICE

I LISTENED to...

....

....

....

I RELATED and CONNECTED to...

....

....

....

I CELEBRATED...

....

....

....

What challenged me today and how can I shift my thinking tomorrow?

....

....

....

SELF CARE

I took care of myself today by...

....

....

....

I drank ☐ glasses of water today

ON A SCALE OF 1 TO 10, HOW DID I DO TODAY?

THRIVING 10
9
8
7
6
5
4
3
2
1 SURVIVING

Today I am at a ☐

REMEMBER

An hour before I go to bed, I will put my work aside (and my phone), breathe and set my intention for tomorrow.

It's a new day!

TODAY'S MINDFUL TIP

Let's build new paths. Use your non-dominant hand for a simple task. Using your opposite hand will strengthen neural connections in your brain, and even grow new ones and more importantly, make you laugh.

MORNING PRACTICE

My INTENTION for today is...

....

....

....

I am THANKFUL for...

....

....

....

Navigate through the noise and simply FOCUS on three to-do's:

1 ....

2 ....

3 ....

Welcome today and RELEASE....

....

....

....

AFTERNOON PRACTICE

I LISTENED to...

....

....

....

I RELATED and CONNECTED to...

....

....

....

I CELEBRATED...

....

....

....

What challenged me today and how can I shift my thinking tomorrow?

....

....

....

SELF CARE

I took care of myself today by...

....

....

....

I drank ☐ glasses of water today

ON A SCALE OF
1 TO 10, HOW DID
I DO TODAY?

THRIVING 10
9
8
7
6
5
4
3
2
1 SURVIVING

Today I am at a ☐

REMEMBER

An hour before I go to bed, I will put my work aside (and my phone), breathe and set my intention for tomorrow.

DAY 111

It's a new day!

TODAY'S MINDFUL TIP

Pay attention to detail. Focus on the way you do one simple task today. Be aware of every single part of the process. It's amazing when you look at every single step of one small moment.

MORNING PRACTICE

My INTENTION for today is...

....

....

....

I am THANKFUL for...

....

....

....

Navigate through the noise and simply FOCUS on three to-do's:

1 ....

2 ....

3 ....

Welcome today and RELEASE....

....

....

....

AFTERNOON PRACTICE

I LISTENED to...

....

....

....

I RELATED and CONNECTED to...

....

....

....

I CELEBRATED...

....

....

....

What challenged me today and how can I shift my thinking tomorrow?

....

....

....

SELF CARE

I took care of myself today by...

....

....

....

I drank ☐ glasses of water today

ON A SCALE OF 1 TO 10, HOW DID I DO TODAY?

THRIVING 10
9
8
7
6
5
4
3
2
1 SURVIVING

Today I am at a ☐

REMEMBER

An hour before I go to bed, I will put my work aside (and my phone), breathe and set my intention for tomorrow.

TODAY'S MINDFUL TIP

Find a quote that serves you and makes you feel uplifted and inspired. Memorize it and repeat to yourself daily.

It's a new day!

MORNING PRACTICE

My INTENTION for today is...

....

....

....

I am THANKFUL for...

....

....

....

Navigate through the noise and simply FOCUS on three to-do's:

1 ....

2 ....

3 ....

Welcome today and RELEASE....

....

....

....

AFTERNOON PRACTICE

I LISTENED to...

....

....

....

I RELATED and CONNECTED to...

....

....

....

I CELEBRATED...

....

....

....

What challenged me today and how can I shift my thinking tomorrow?

....

....

....

SELF CARE

I took care of myself today by...

....

....

I drank ☐ glasses of water today

ON A SCALE OF 1 TO 10, HOW DID I DO TODAY?

THRIVING 10
9
8
7
6
5
4
3
2
1 SURVIVING

Today I am at a ☐

REMEMBER

An hour before I go to bed, I will put my work aside (and my phone), breathe and set my intention for tomorrow.

It's a new day!

MORNING PRACTICE

My INTENTION for today is...

....

....

....

I am THANKFUL for...

....

....

....

Navigate through the noise and simply FOCUS on three to-do's:

1 ....

2 ....

3 ....

Welcome today and RELEASE....

....

....

....

AFTERNOON PRACTICE

I LISTENED to...

....

....

....

I RELATED and CONNECTED to...

....

....

....

I CELEBRATED...

....

....

....

What challenged me today and how can I shift my thinking tomorrow?

....

....

....

SELF CARE

I took care of myself today by...

....

....

....

I drank ☐ glasses of water today

ON A SCALE OF 1 TO 10, HOW DID I DO TODAY?

THRIVING 10

9

8

7

6

5

4

3

2

1 SURVIVING

Today I am at a ☐

REMEMBER

An hour before I go to bed, I will put my work aside (and my phone), breathe and set my intention for tomorrow.

It's a new day!

TODAY'S MINDFUL TIP

Drive less, walk more. The health benefits are enormous. Walking can significantly reduce stress, increase your energy, saves you money, is good for the environment and allows you time to stop and smell the roses (if you want).

MORNING PRACTICE

My INTENTION for today is...

....

....

....

I am THANKFUL for...

....

....

....

Navigate through the noise and simply FOCUS on three to-do's:

1 ....

2 ....

3 ....

Welcome today and RELEASE....

....

....

....

AFTERNOON PRACTICE

I LISTENED to...

_____

_____

_____

I RELATED and CONNECTED to...

_____

_____

_____

I CELEBRATED...

_____

_____

_____

What challenged me today and how can I shift my thinking tomorrow?

_____

_____

SELF CARE

I took care of myself today by...

_____

_____

I drank ☐ glasses of water today

ON A SCALE OF 1 TO 10, HOW DID I DO TODAY?

THRIVING 10
9
8
7
6
5
4
3
2
1 SURVIVING

Today I am at a ☐

REMEMBER

An hour before I go to bed, I will put my work aside (and my phone), breathe and set my intention for tomorrow.

It's a new day!

TODAY'S
MINDFUL TIP

Your space is your sanctuary. Create a space that is calm, inviting and inclusive and use it often.

MORNING PRACTICE

My INTENTION for today is...

....

....

....

I am THANKFUL for...

....

....

....

Navigate through the noise and simply FOCUS on three to-do's:

1 ....

2 ....

3 ....

Welcome today and RELEASE....

....

....

....

AFTERNOON PRACTICE

I LISTENED to...

....

....

....

I RELATED and CONNECTED to...

....

....

....

I CELEBRATED...

....

....

....

What challenged me today and how can I shift my thinking tomorrow?

....

....

....

SELF CARE

I took care of myself today by...

....

....

I drank ☐ glasses of water today

ON A SCALE OF 1 TO 10, HOW DID I DO TODAY?

THRIVING   10

9

8

7

6

5

4

3

2

1   SURVIVING

Today I am at a ☐

REMEMBER

An hour before I go to bed, I will put my work aside (and my phone), breathe and set my intention for tomorrow.

It's a new day!

MORNING PRACTICE

My INTENTION for today is...

....

....

....

I am THANKFUL for...

....

....

....

Navigate through the noise and simply FOCUS on three to-do's:

1 ....

2 ....

3 ....

Welcome today and RELEASE....

....

....

....

AFTERNOON PRACTICE

I LISTENED to...

_____

_____

_____

I RELATED and CONNECTED to...

_____

_____

_____

I CELEBRATED...

_____

_____

_____

What challenged me today and how can I shift my
thinking tomorrow?

_____

_____

SELF CARE

I took care of myself today by...

_____

_____

I drank ☐ glasses of water today

ON A SCALE OF I TO IO, HOW DID I DO TODAY?

THRIVING 10
9
8
7
6
5
4
3
2
1 SURVIVING

Today I am at a ☐

REMEMBER

An hour before I go to bed,
I will put my work aside
(and my phone), breathe
and set my intention for
tomorrow.

DAY 117

TODAY'S MINDFUL TIP

Go on a treasure hunt.
Take a few minutes to
look around and create
a top 10 treasure list.
There are treasures
everywhere.

It's a new day!

MORNING PRACTICE

My INTENTION for today is...

....

....

....

I am THANKFUL for...

....

....

....

Navigate through the noise and simply FOCUS on three to-do's:

1 ....

2 ....

3 ....

Welcome today and RELEASE....

....

....

....

AFTERNOON PRACTICE

I LISTENED to...

_____

_____

_____

I RELATED and CONNECTED to...

_____

_____

_____

I CELEBRATED...

_____

_____

_____

What challenged me today and how can I shift my thinking tomorrow?

_____

_____

_____

SELF CARE

I took care of myself today by...

_____

_____

_____

I drank ☐ glasses of water today

ON A SCALE OF 1 TO 10, HOW DID I DO TODAY?

THRIVING 10

9

8

7

6

5

4

3

2

1 SURVIVING

Today I am at a ☐

REMEMBER

An hour before I go to bed, I will put my work aside (and my phone), breathe and set my intention for tomorrow.

It's a new day!

TODAY'S MINDFUL TIP

Patience is a virtue.
Today, make it a priority
to bring more patience
to a conversation or
relationship.

MORNING PRACTICE

My INTENTION for today is...

....

....

....

I am THANKFUL for...

....

....

....

Navigate through the noise and simply FOCUS on
three to-do's:

1 ....

2 ....

3 ....

Welcome today and RELEASE....

....

....

....

AFTERNOON PRACTICE

I LISTENED to...

....

....

....

I RELATED and CONNECTED to...

....

....

....

I CELEBRATED...

....

....

....

What challenged me today and how can I shift my thinking tomorrow?

....

....

....

SELF CARE

I took care of myself today by...

....

....

....

I drank ☐ glasses of water today

ON A SCALE OF 1 TO 10, HOW DID I DO TODAY?

THRIVING 10
9
8
7
6
5
4
3
2
1 SURVIVING

Today I am at a ☐

REMEMBER

An hour before I go to bed, I will put my work aside (and my phone), breathe and set my intention for tomorrow.

DAY 119

It's a new day!

TODAY'S MINDFUL TIP

Are you all in? When you truly give it your all, nothing is left on the table, leaving no room for regret.

MORNING PRACTICE

My INTENTION for today is...

....

....

....

I am THANKFUL for...

....

....

....

Navigate through the noise and simply FOCUS on three to-do's:

1 ....

2 ....

3 ....

Welcome today and RELEASE....

....

....

....

AFTERNOON PRACTICE

I LISTENED to...

....

....

....

I RELATED and CONNECTED to...

....

....

....

I CELEBRATED...

....

....

....

What challenged me today and how can I shift my thinking tomorrow?

....

....

....

SELF CARE

I took care of myself today by...

....

....

....

I drank ☐ glasses of water today

ON A SCALE OF 1 TO 10, HOW DID I DO TODAY?

THRIVING 10
9
8
7
6
5
4
3
2
1 SURVIVING

Today I am at a ☐

REMEMBER

An hour before I go to bed, I will put my work aside (and my phone), breathe and set my intention for tomorrow.

It's a new day!

MORNING PRACTICE

My INTENTION for today is...

....

....

....

I am THANKFUL for...

....

....

....

Navigate through the noise and simply FOCUS on three to-do's:

1 ....

2 ....

3 ....

Welcome today and RELEASE....

....

....

....

AFTERNOON PRACTICE

I LISTENED to...

....

....

....

I RELATED and CONNECTED to...

....

....

....

I CELEBRATED...

....

....

....

What challenged me today and how can I shift my thinking tomorrow?

....

....

....

SELF CARE

I took care of myself today by...

....

....

....

I drank ☐ glasses of water today

ON A SCALE OF 1 TO 10, HOW DID I DO TODAY?

THRIVING 10

9

8

7

6

5

4

3

2

1 SURVIVING

Today I am at a ☐

REMEMBER

An hour before I go to bed, I will put my work aside (and my phone), breathe and set my intention for tomorrow.

It's a new day!

MORNING PRACTICE

My INTENTION for today is...

....
....
....

I am THANKFUL for...

....
....
....

Navigate through the noise and simply FOCUS on three to-do's:

1 ....

2 ....

3 ....

Welcome today and RELEASE....

....
....
....

AFTERNOON PRACTICE

I LISTENED to...

....

....

....

I RELATED and CONNECTED to...

....

....

....

I CELEBRATED...

....

....

....

What challenged me today and how can I shift my thinking tomorrow?

....

....

....

SELF CARE

I took care of myself today by...

....

....

....

I drank ☐ glasses of water today

ON A SCALE OF 1 TO 10, HOW DID I DO TODAY?

THRIVING 10

9

8

7

6

5

4

3

2

1 SURVIVING

Today I am at a ☐

REMEMBER

An hour before I go to bed, I will put my work aside (and my phone), breathe and set my intention for tomorrow.

It's a new day!

TODAY'S
MINDFUL TIP

The sound of silence.
On your way to work
today, spend it in
silence. No music, no
phone, just you settling
in with your mind and
body.

MORNING PRACTICE

My INTENTION for today is...

I am THANKFUL for...

Navigate through the noise and simply FOCUS on
three to-do's:

1

2

3

Welcome today and RELEASE....

AFTERNOON PRACTICE

I LISTENED to...

....

....

....

I RELATED and CONNECTED to...

....

....

....

I CELEBRATED...

....

....

....

What challenged me today and how can I shift my thinking tomorrow?

....

....

....

SELF CARE

I took care of myself today by...

....

....

....

I drank [   ] glasses of water today

ON A SCALE OF 1 TO 10, HOW DID I DO TODAY?

THRIVING 10

9

8

7

6

5

4

3

2

1 SURVIVING

Today I am at a [   ]

REMEMBER

An hour before I go to bed, I will put my work aside (and my phone), breathe and set my intention for tomorrow.

It's a new day!

TODAY'S MINDFUL TIP

"Always be a little kinder than necessary."
—JM Barrie

MORNING PRACTICE

My INTENTION for today is...

....

....

....

I am THANKFUL for...

....

....

....

Navigate through the noise and simply FOCUS on three to-do's:

1 ....

2 ....

3 ....

Welcome today and RELEASE....

....

....

....

AFTERNOON PRACTICE

I LISTENED to...

....

....

....

I RELATED and CONNECTED to...

....

....

....

I CELEBRATED...

....

....

....

What challenged me today and how can I shift my thinking tomorrow?

....

....

....

SELF CARE

I took care of myself today by...

....

....

....

I drank ☐ glasses of water today

ON A SCALE OF 1 TO 10, HOW DID I DO TODAY?

THRIVING 10

9

8

7

6

5

4

3

2

1 SURVIVING

Today I am at a ☐

REMEMBER

An hour before I go to bed, I will put my work aside (and my phone), breathe and set my intention for tomorrow.

It's a new day!

TODAY'S MINDFUL TIP

Take time today to color or doodle. Use your favorite colors and enjoy the mindfulness of being carefree. No rules, no expectations and yes, you can color outside the lines. Now hang up your masterpiece.

MORNING PRACTICE

My INTENTION for today is...

....

....

....

I am THANKFUL for...

....

....

....

Navigate through the noise and simply FOCUS on three to-do's:

1 ....

2 ....

3 ....

Welcome today and RELEASE....

....

....

....

AFTERNOON PRACTICE

I LISTENED to...

....

....

....

I RELATED and CONNECTED to...

....

....

....

I CELEBRATED...

....

....

....

What challenged me today and how can I shift my thinking tomorrow?

....

....

....

SELF CARE

I took care of myself today by...

....

....

....

I drank ☐ glasses of water today

ON A SCALE OF 1 TO 10, HOW DID I DO TODAY?

THRIVING 10
9
8
7
6
5
4
3
2
1 SURVIVING

Today I am at a ☐

REMEMBER

An hour before I go to bed, I will put my work aside (and my phone), breathe and set my intention for tomorrow.

Resilience Reflection

EMOTIONAL
RESILIENCE
IS...

a person's ability
to recover after a
setback and to thrive
in the midst
of challenges,
not just survive.

CHECK IN

Reflecting on the last 25 days, how well did I
implement my daily practices (*before school,
after school, self-care, mindfulness*)?

What went WELL?

....

....

....

....

What did I STRUGGLE with?

....

....

....

....

ON ANY GIVEN DAY we experience a myriad of highs and lows. While some emotional resilience comes naturally to us, we all have the ability to increase our capacity over time and thrive.

Look back on the past 25 days. On a scale of 1 to 10, where do I **FIND MYSELF** on this line? *Add up your daily scores and divide by 25 to indicate your score.* I AM a ☐

1 ——— 2 ——— 3 ——— 4 ——— 5 ——— 6 ——— 7 ——— 8 ——— 9 ——— 10 →

SURVIVING   THRIVING

What **ADJUSTMENTS** can I make for the next 25 days to **THRIVE**?

....

....

....

....

Keep Going!

You've Got This!

It's a new day!

MORNING PRACTICE

My INTENTION for today is...

....
....
....

I am THANKFUL for...

....
....
....

Navigate through the noise and simply FOCUS on
three to-do's:

1 ....

2 ....

3 ....

Welcome today and RELEASE....

....
....
....

AFTERNOON PRACTICE

I LISTENED to...

....

....

....

I RELATED and CONNECTED to...

....

....

....

I CELEBRATED...

....

....

....

What challenged me today and how can I shift my thinking tomorrow?

....

....

....

SELF CARE

I took care of myself today by...

....

....

....

I drank ☐ glasses of water today

ON A SCALE OF
I TO 10, HOW DID
I DO TODAY?

THRIVING 10

9

8

7

6

5

4

3

2

1 SURVIVING

Today I am at a ☐

REMEMBER

An hour before I go to bed, I will put my work aside (and my phone), breathe and set my intention for tomorrow.

It's a new day!

TODAY'S MINDFUL TIP

Get into a comfortable position, take three mindful breaths, close your eyes or look down and visualize what a perfect day would look like today and now consciously live that day.

MORNING PRACTICE

My INTENTION for today is...

....

....

....

I am THANKFUL for...

....

....

....

Navigate through the noise and simply FOCUS on three to-do's:

1 ....

2 ....

3 ....

Welcome today and RELEASE....

....

....

....

AFTERNOON PRACTICE

I LISTENED to...

....

....

....

I RELATED and CONNECTED to...

....

....

....

I CELEBRATED...

....

....

....

What challenged me today and how can I shift my thinking tomorrow?

....

....

....

SELF CARE

I took care of myself today by...

....

....

....

I drank ☐ glasses of water today

ON A SCALE OF 1 TO 10, HOW DID I DO TODAY?

THRIVING 10

9

8

7

6

5

4

3

2

1 SURVIVING

Today I am at a ☐

REMEMBER

An hour before I go to bed, I will put my work aside (and my phone), breathe and set my intention for tomorrow.

It's a new day!

TODAY'S MINDFUL TIP

Pay it forward today. Paying it **forward** inspires generosity and compassion and more importantly, it instills a sense of purpose in humanity.

MORNING PRACTICE

My INTENTION for today is...

....
....
....

I am THANKFUL for...

....
....
....

Navigate through the noise and simply FOCUS on three to-do's:

1 ....

2 ....

3 ....

Welcome today and RELEASE....

....
....
....

AFTERNOON PRACTICE

I LISTENED to...

....

....

....

I RELATED and CONNECTED to...

....

....

....

I CELEBRATED...

....

....

....

What challenged me today and how can I shift my thinking tomorrow?

....

....

....

SELF CARE

I took care of myself today by...

....

....

....

I drank ☐ glasses of water today

ON A SCALE OF
1 TO 10, HOW DID
I DO TODAY?

THRIVING 10
9
8
7
6
5
4
3
2
1 SURVIVING

Today I am at a ☐

REMEMBER

An hour before I go to bed,
I will put my work aside
(and my phone), breathe
and set my intention for
tomorrow.

It's a new day!

TODAY'S MINDFUL TIP

Take time to watch **Gratitude: The Short Film by Louie Schwartzberg**. It is worth every single minute!

MORNING PRACTICE

My INTENTION for today is...

I am THANKFUL for...

Navigate through the noise and simply FOCUS on three to-do's:

1

2

3

Welcome today and RELEASE....

AFTERNOON PRACTICE

I LISTENED to...

_____

_____

_____

I RELATED and CONNECTED to...

_____

_____

_____

I CELEBRATED...

_____

_____

_____

What challenged me today and how can I shift my thinking tomorrow?

_____

_____

_____

SELF CARE

I took care of myself today by...

_____

_____

_____

I drank ☐ glasses of water today

ON A SCALE OF 1 TO 10, HOW DID I DO TODAY?

THRIVING 10
9
8
7
6
5
4
3
2
1 SURVIVING

Today I am at a ☐

REMEMBER

An hour before I go to bed, I will put my work aside (and my phone), breathe and set my intention for tomorrow.

It's a new day!

MORNING PRACTICE

My INTENTION for today is...

_____
_____
_____

I am THANKFUL for...

_____
_____
_____

Navigate through the noise and simply FOCUS on three to-do's:

1 _____

2 _____

3 _____

Welcome today and RELEASE....

_____
_____
_____

AFTERNOON PRACTICE

I LISTENED to...

....

....

....

I RELATED and CONNECTED to...

....

....

....

I CELEBRATED...

....

....

....

What challenged me today and how can I shift my
thinking tomorrow?

....

....

....

SELF CARE

I took care of myself today by...

....

....

....

I drank ☐ glasses of water today

ON A SCALE OF I TO 10, HOW DID I DO TODAY?

THRIVING 10
9
8
7
6
5
4
3
2
1 SURVIVING

Today I am at a ☐

REMEMBER

An hour before I go to bed,
I will put my work aside
(and my phone), breathe
and set my intention for
tomorrow.

DAY 131

It's a new day!

TODAY'S MINDFUL TIP

Get your hands dirty. Build, garden, craft, paint etc. When you engage in hands-on activities centered around creating, studies show significant improvement in emotional resilience and increased connectivity in the brain (how different parts of the brain work together).

MORNING PRACTICE

My INTENTION for today is...

....

....

....

I am THANKFUL for...

....

....

....

Navigate through the noise and simply FOCUS on three to-do's:

1 ....

2 ....

3 ....

Welcome today and RELEASE....

....

....

....

AFTERNOON PRACTICE

I LISTENED to...

....

....

....

I RELATED and CONNECTED to...

....

....

....

I CELEBRATED...

....

....

....

What challenged me today and how can I shift my thinking tomorrow?

....

....

....

SELF CARE

I took care of myself today by...

....

....

....

I drank ☐ glasses of water today

ON A SCALE OF 1 TO 10, HOW DID I DO TODAY?

THRIVING 10

9

8

7

6

5

4

3

2

1 SURVIVING

Today I am at a ☐

REMEMBER

An hour before I go to bed, I will put my work aside (and my phone), breathe and set my intention for tomorrow.

It's a new day!

TODAY'S MINDFUL TIP

Do something you loved to do as a child. Skip, play hop scotch, go biking with a friend. Going down memory lane is good for you. Nostalgia has been shown to counteract loneliness, boredom and anxiety and makes you feel safe and loved.

MORNING PRACTICE

My INTENTION for today is...

....
....
....

I am THANKFUL for...

....
....
....

Navigate through the noise and simply FOCUS on three to-do's:

1 ....

2 ....

3 ....

Welcome today and RELEASE....

....
....
....

AFTERNOON PRACTICE

I LISTENED to...

....

....

....

I RELATED and CONNECTED to...

....

....

....

I CELEBRATED...

....

....

....

What challenged me today and how can I shift my thinking tomorrow?

....

....

....

SELF CARE

I took care of myself today by...

....

....

....

I drank ☐ glasses of water today

ON A SCALE OF 1 TO 10, HOW DID I DO TODAY?

THRIVING 10
9
8
7
6
5
4
3
2
1 SURVIVING

Today I am at a ☐

REMEMBER

An hour before I go to bed, I will put my work aside (and my phone), breathe and set my intention for tomorrow.

It's a new day!

MORNING PRACTICE

My INTENTION for today is...

....

....

....

I am THANKFUL for...

....

....

....

Navigate through the noise and simply FOCUS on three to-do's:

1 ....

2 ....

3 ....

Welcome today and RELEASE....

....

....

....

AFTERNOON PRACTICE

I LISTENED to...

....

....

....

I RELATED and CONNECTED to...

....

....

....

I CELEBRATED...

....

....

....

What challenged me today and how can I shift my thinking tomorrow?

....

....

....

SELF CARE

I took care of myself today by...

....

....

....

I drank ☐ glasses of water today

ON A SCALE OF
1 TO 10, HOW DID
I DO TODAY?

THRIVING 10
9
8
7
6
5
4
3
2
1 SURVIVING

Today I am at a ☐

REMEMBER
An hour before I go to bed, I will put my work aside (and my phone), breathe and set my intention for tomorrow.

DAY 134

It's a new day!

TODAY'S MINDFUL TIP

Fix something today that is broken (metaphorically or physically). We live in a world where we replace things when they break instead of taking the time and effort to repair them. When we do carve out that time, we have a sense of pride and a new connection with what has been broken.

MORNING PRACTICE

My INTENTION for today is...

....

....

....

I am THANKFUL for...

....

....

....

Navigate through the noise and simply FOCUS on three to-do's:

1 ....

2 ....

3 ....

Welcome today and RELEASE....

....

....

....

AFTERNOON PRACTICE

I LISTENED to...

_____

_____

_____

I RELATED and CONNECTED to...

_____

_____

_____

I CELEBRATED...

_____

_____

_____

What challenged me today and how can I shift my thinking tomorrow?

_____

_____

_____

SELF CARE

I took care of myself today by...

_____

_____

_____

I drank ⬜ glasses of water today

ON A SCALE OF I TO 10, HOW DID I DO TODAY?

THRIVING 10

9

8

7

6

5

4

3

2

1 SURVIVING

Today I am at a ⬜

REMEMBER

An hour before I go to bed, I will put my work aside (and my phone), breathe and set my intention for tomorrow.

It's a new day!

TODAY'S
MINDFUL TIP

Replace your "should"
with want. When we
stop and say what
do I really want, the
uncertainty and
unsettling "should" takes
a back seat.

MORNING PRACTICE

My INTENTION for today is...

....

....

....

I am THANKFUL for...

....

....

....

Navigate through the noise and simply FOCUS on three to-do's:

1 ....

2 ....

3 ....

Welcome today and RELEASE....

....

....

....

AFTERNOON PRACTICE

I LISTENED to...

....

....

....

I RELATED and CONNECTED to...

....

....

....

I CELEBRATED...

....

....

....

What challenged me today and how can I shift my thinking tomorrow?

....

....

....

SELF CARE

I took care of myself today by...

....

....

I drank ☐ glasses of water today

ON A SCALE OF 1 TO 10, HOW DID I DO TODAY?

THRIVING 10

9

8

7

6

5

4

3

2

1 SURVIVING

Today I am at a ☐

REMEMBER

An hour before I go to bed, I will put my work aside (and my phone), breathe and set my intention for tomorrow.

It's a new day!

MORNING PRACTICE

My INTENTION for today is...

....

....

....

I am THANKFUL for...

....

....

....

Navigate through the noise and simply FOCUS on three to-do's:

1 ....

2 ....

3 ....

Welcome today and RELEASE....

....

....

....

AFTERNOON PRACTICE

I **LISTENED** to...

....

....

....

I **RELATED** and **CONNECTED** to...

....

....

....

I **CELEBRATED**...

....

....

....

What challenged me today and how can I shift my thinking tomorrow?

....

....

....

SELF CARE

I took care of myself today by...

....

....

....

I drank ☐ glasses of water today

ON A SCALE OF 1 TO 10, HOW DID I DO TODAY?

THRIVING 10

9

8

7

6

5

4

3

2

1 SURVIVING

Today I am at a ☐

REMEMBER

An hour before I go to bed, I will put my work aside (and my phone), breathe and set my intention for tomorrow.

It's a new day!

TODAY'S MINDFUL TIP

Get your asset focused radar out. Pick three individuals and list five assets they possess. Now tell them. **Challenge:** Pick three individuals that you may struggle with and list five assets. Now tell them.

MORNING PRACTICE

My INTENTION for today is...

....

....

....

I am THANKFUL for...

....

....

....

Navigate through the noise and simply FOCUS on three to-do's:

1 ....

2 ....

3 ....

Welcome today and RELEASE....

....

....

....

AFTERNOON PRACTICE

I LISTENED to...

....

....

....

I RELATED and CONNECTED to...

....

....

....

I CELEBRATED...

....

....

....

What challenged me today and how can I shift my thinking tomorrow?

....

....

....

SELF CARE

I took care of myself today by...

....

....

....

I drank ☐ glasses of water today

ON A SCALE OF 1 TO 10, HOW DID I DO TODAY?

THRIVING 10

9

8

7

6

5

4

3

2

1 SURVIVING

Today I am at a ☐

REMEMBER

An hour before I go to bed, I will put my work aside (and my phone), breathe and set my intention for tomorrow.

It's a new day!

TODAY'S MINDFUL TIP

"Today might be the day a kid reminds you about 20 years from now. Make it awesome."

—@ideaguy42

MORNING PRACTICE

My INTENTION for today is...

....

....

....

I am THANKFUL for...

....

....

....

Navigate through the noise and simply FOCUS on three to-do's:

1 ....

2 ....

3 ....

Welcome today and RELEASE....

....

....

....

AFTERNOON PRACTICE

I LISTENED to...

....

....

....

I RELATED and CONNECTED to...

....

....

....

I CELEBRATED...

....

....

....

What challenged me today and how can I shift my thinking tomorrow?

....

....

....

SELF CARE

I took care of myself today by...

....

....

....

I drank ☐ glasses of water today

ON A SCALE OF 1 TO 10, HOW DID I DO TODAY?

THRIVING 10
9
8
7
6
5
4
3
2
1 SURVIVING

Today I am at a ☐

REMEMBER

An hour before I go to bed, I will put my work aside (and my phone), breathe and set my intention for tomorrow.

It's a new day!

TODAY'S MINDFUL TIP

Think outside the box. Today, dare to do something different that is a little out of the norm. Be creative, have fun and enjoy the process. No need to justify your actions, just enjoy the freedom of choice.

MORNING PRACTICE

My INTENTION for today is...

....

....

....

I am THANKFUL for...

....

....

....

Navigate through the noise and simply FOCUS on three to-do's:

1 ....

2 ....

3 ....

Welcome today and RELEASE....

....

....

....

AFTERNOON PRACTICE

I LISTENED to...

....

....

....

I RELATED and CONNECTED to...

....

....

....

I CELEBRATED...

....

....

....

What challenged me today and how can I shift my thinking tomorrow?

....

....

....

SELF CARE

I took care of myself today by...

....

....

....

I drank ☐ glasses of water today

ON A SCALE OF 1 TO 10, HOW DID I DO TODAY?

THRIVING 10
9
8
7
6
5
4
3
2
1 SURVIVING

Today I am at a ☐

REMEMBER

An hour before I go to bed, I will put my work aside (and my phone), breathe and set my intention for tomorrow.

DAY 140

It's a new day!

TODAY'S MINDFUL TIP

We are what we choose. Answer the following questions: What are you focusing on right now? Is it making you feel good? Are you getting what you want from where you are putting your attention? Loving life is a choice. When you feel yourself going to a place that does not serve you, it's time to shift the focus.

MORNING PRACTICE

My INTENTION for today is...

....

....

....

I am THANKFUL for...

....

....

....

Navigate through the noise and simply FOCUS on three to-do's:

1 ....

2 ....

3 ....

Welcome today and RELEASE....

....

....

....

AFTERNOON PRACTICE

I LISTENED to...

....

....

....

I RELATED and CONNECTED to...

....

....

....

I CELEBRATED...

....

....

....

What challenged me today and how can I shift my thinking tomorrow?

....

....

....

SELF CARE

I took care of myself today by...

....

....

....

I drank ☐ glasses of water today

ON A SCALE OF 1 TO 10, HOW DID I DO TODAY?

THRIVING 10

9

8

7

6

5

4

3

2

1 SURVIVING

Today I am at a ☐

REMEMBER

An hour before I go to bed, I will put my work aside (and my phone), breathe and set my intention for tomorrow.

It's a new day!

MORNING PRACTICE

My INTENTION for today is...

I am THANKFUL for...

Navigate through the noise and simply FOCUS on three to-do's:

1

2

3

Welcome today and RELEASE....

AFTERNOON PRACTICE

I LISTENED to...

....

....

....

I RELATED and CONNECTED to...

....

....

....

I CELEBRATED...

....

....

....

What challenged me today and how can I shift my thinking tomorrow?

....

....

....

SELF CARE

I took care of myself today by...

....

....

....

I drank ☐ glasses of water today

ON A SCALE OF 1 TO 10, HOW DID I DO TODAY?

THRIVING 10

9

8

7

6

5

4

3

2

1 SURVIVING

Today I am at a ☐

REMEMBER

An hour before I go to bed, I will put my work aside (and my phone), breathe and set my intention for tomorrow.

It's a new day!

TODAY'S MINDFUL TIP

A picture is worth a thousand words. Pick five of your favorite pictures stored on your phone. Print them out and post them on your wall or in a frame that is visible to you during the day.

MORNING PRACTICE

My INTENTION for today is...

....

....

....

I am THANKFUL for...

....

....

....

Navigate through the noise and simply FOCUS on three to-do's:

1 ....

2 ....

3 ....

Welcome today and RELEASE....

....

....

....

AFTERNOON PRACTICE

I LISTENED to...

....

....

....

I RELATED and CONNECTED to...

....

....

....

I CELEBRATED...

....

....

....

What challenged me today and how can I shift my thinking tomorrow?

....

....

....

SELF CARE

I took care of myself today by...

....

....

....

I drank [ ] glasses of water today

ON A SCALE OF 1 TO 10, HOW DID I DO TODAY?

THRIVING 10
9
8
7
6
5
4
3
2
1 SURVIVING

Today I am at a [ ]

REMEMBER

An hour before I go to bed, I will put my work aside (and my phone), breathe and set my intention for tomorrow.

It's a new day!

MORNING PRACTICE

My INTENTION for today is...

....

....

....

I am THANKFUL for...

....

....

....

Navigate through the noise and simply FOCUS on three to-do's:

1 ....

2 ....

3 ....

Welcome today and RELEASE....

....

....

....

AFTERNOON PRACTICE

I LISTENED to...

....

....

....

I RELATED and CONNECTED to...

....

....

....

I CELEBRATED...

....

....

....

What challenged me today and how can I shift my thinking tomorrow?

....

....

....

SELF CARE

I took care of myself today by...

....

....

....

I drank ☐ glasses of water today

ON A SCALE OF 1 TO 10, HOW DID I DO TODAY?

THRIVING 10
9
8
7
6
5
4
3
2
1 SURVIVING

Today I am at a ☐

REMEMBER

An hour before I go to bed, I will put my work aside (and my phone), breathe and set my intention for tomorrow.

It's a new day!

TODAY'S MINDFUL TIP

Today breathe deeply before you speak and only speak with kindness.

MORNING PRACTICE

My INTENTION for today is...

....

....

....

I am THANKFUL for...

....

....

....

Navigate through the noise and simply FOCUS on three to-do's:

1 ....

2 ....

3 ....

Welcome today and RELEASE....

....

....

....

AFTERNOON PRACTICE

I LISTENED to...

....

....

....

I RELATED and CONNECTED to...

....

....

....

I CELEBRATED...

....

....

....

What challenged me today and how can I shift my thinking tomorrow?

....

....

....

SELF CARE

I took care of myself today by...

....

....

....

I drank ☐ glasses of water today

ON A SCALE OF 1 TO 10, HOW DID I DO TODAY?

THRIVING 10

9

8

7

6

5

4

3

2

1 SURVIVING

Today I am at a ☐

REMEMBER

An hour before I go to bed, I will put my work aside (and my phone), breathe and set my intention for tomorrow.

DAY 145

It's a new day!

MORNING PRACTICE

My INTENTION for today is...

....

....

....

I am THANKFUL for...

....

....

....

Navigate through the noise and simply FOCUS on three to-do's:

1 ....

2 ....

3 ....

Welcome today and RELEASE....

....

....

....

TODAY'S MINDFUL TIP

Create a list of daily positive affirmations. For example: I am strong, I am courageous...

Daily affirmations are designed to alter the beliefs about ourselves so we think more positively and motivate us. Studies have shown people that practice positive affirmations are happier, more optimistic and have a clearer perspective on life.

AFTERNOON PRACTICE

I LISTENED to...

....

....

....

I RELATED and CONNECTED to...

....

....

....

I CELEBRATED...

....

....

....

What challenged me today and how can I shift my thinking tomorrow?

....

....

....

SELF CARE

I took care of myself today by...

....

....

....

I drank ☐ glasses of water today

ON A SCALE OF 1 TO 10, HOW DID I DO TODAY?

THRIVING 10
9
8
7
6
5
4
3
2
1 SURVIVING

Today I am at a ☐

REMEMBER

An hour before I go to bed, I will put my work aside (and my phone), breathe and set my intention for tomorrow.

DAY 146

It's a new day!

MORNING PRACTICE

My INTENTION for today is...

I am THANKFUL for...

Navigate through the noise and simply FOCUS on three to-do's:

1

2

3

Welcome today and RELEASE....

AFTERNOON PRACTICE

I LISTENED to...

....

....

....

I RELATED and CONNECTED to...

....

....

....

I CELEBRATED...

....

....

....

What challenged me today and how can I shift my thinking tomorrow?

....

....

....

SELF CARE

I took care of myself today by...

....

....

I drank ☐ glasses of water today

ON A SCALE OF 1 TO 10, HOW DID I DO TODAY?

THRIVING 10
9
8
7
6
5
4
3
2
1 SURVIVING

Today I am at a ☐

REMEMBER

An hour before I go to bed, I will put my work aside (and my phone), breathe and set my intention for tomorrow.

DAY 147

It's a new day!

TODAY'S MINDFUL TIP

Work toward your goals harder than you ever have today.

MORNING PRACTICE

My INTENTION for today is...

....

....

....

I am THANKFUL for...

....

....

....

Navigate through the noise and simply FOCUS on three to-do's:

1 ....

2 ....

3 ....

Welcome today and RELEASE....

....

....

....

AFTERNOON PRACTICE

I LISTENED to...

....

....

....

I RELATED and CONNECTED to...

....

....

....

I CELEBRATED...

....

....

....

What challenged me today and how can I shift my thinking tomorrow?

....

....

....

SELF CARE

I took care of myself today by...

....

....

....

I drank [ ] glasses of water today

ON A SCALE OF 1 TO 10, HOW DID I DO TODAY?

THRIVING 10
9
8
7
6
5
4
3
2
1 SURVIVING

Today I am at a [ ]

REMEMBER

An hour before I go to bed, I will put my work aside (and my phone), breathe and set my intention for tomorrow.

It's a new day!

TODAY'S MINDFUL TIP

Mindfully clean your home. Instead of racing through the chores, carve out time, turn off your phone and other distractions, and find your focus on cleaning and nothing else. When you apply mindfulness principles to cleaning and organizing your home, you not only end up doing a better job (a clean and organized home feels good), but you learn how to find meaning in chores and ordinary moments.

MORNING PRACTICE

My INTENTION for today is...

....

....

....

I am THANKFUL for...

....

....

Navigate through the noise and simply FOCUS on three to-do's:

1 ....

2 ....

3 ....

Welcome today and RELEASE....

....

....

....

AFTERNOON PRACTICE

I LISTENED to...

....

....

....

I RELATED and CONNECTED to...

....

....

....

I CELEBRATED...

....

....

....

What challenged me today and how can I shift my thinking tomorrow?

....

....

....

SELF CARE

I took care of myself today by...

....

....

....

I drank ☐ glasses of water today

ON A SCALE OF 1 TO 10, HOW DID I DO TODAY?

THRIVING 10
9
8
7
6
5
4
3
2
1 SURVIVING

Today I am at a ☐

REMEMBER

An hour before I go to bed, I will put my work aside (and my phone), breathe and set my intention for tomorrow.

It's a new day!

TODAY'S MINDFUL TIP

Smile and say hello to the first ten people you come in contact with today.

MORNING PRACTICE

My INTENTION for today is...

....

....

....

I am THANKFUL for...

....

....

....

Navigate through the noise and simply FOCUS on three to-do's:

1 ....

2 ....

3 ....

Welcome today and RELEASE....

....

....

....

AFTERNOON PRACTICE

I LISTENED to...

_____

_____

_____

I RELATED and CONNECTED to...

_____

_____

_____

I CELEBRATED...

_____

_____

_____

What challenged me today and how can I shift my thinking tomorrow?

_____

_____

_____

SELF CARE

I took care of myself today by...

_____

_____

I drank ☐ glasses of water today

ON A SCALE OF 1 TO 10, HOW DID I DO TODAY?

↑

THRIVING 10

9

8

7

6

5

4

3

2

1 SURVIVING

Today I am at a ☐

REMEMBER

An hour before I go to bed, I will put my work aside (and my phone), breathe and set my intention for tomorrow.

Resilience Reflection

EMOTIONAL RESILIENCE IS...

a person's ability to recover after a setback and to thrive in the midst of challenges, not just survive.

CHECK IN

Reflecting on the last 25 days, how well did I implement my daily practices (*before school, after school, self-care, mindfulness*)?

What went WELL?

....

....

....

....

What did I STRUGGLE with?

....

....

....

....

ON ANY GIVEN DAY we experience a myriad of highs and lows. While some emotional resilience comes naturally to us, we all have the ability to increase our capacity over time and thrive.

Look back on the past 25 days. On a scale of 1 to 10, where do I FIND MYSELF on this line? *Add up your daily scores and divide by 25 to indicate your score.* I AM a ☐

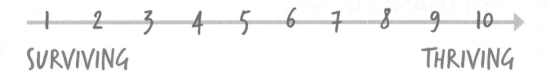

1   2   3   4   5   6   7   8   9   10

SURVIVING   THRIVING

What ADJUSTMENTS can I make for the next 25 days to THRIVE?

....

....

....

....

Keep Going!

You've Got This!

It's a new day!

TODAY'S MINDFUL TIP

Are you facing some noise today? Can you bring your focus back to what your intentions were today? Being able to focus is a discipline that needs practice and lots of reps. Clear your mind of anything other than what your intention was today. Try to hold that focus for sixty seconds. With practice we can learn how to focus on what is important and let the rest of the noise go.

MORNING PRACTICE

My INTENTION for today is...

....

....

....

I am THANKFUL for...

....

....

....

Navigate through the noise and simply FOCUS on three to-do's:

1 ....

2 ....

3 ....

Welcome today and RELEASE....

....

....

....

AFTERNOON PRACTICE

I LISTENED to...

....

....

....

I RELATED and CONNECTED to...

....

....

....

I CELEBRATED...

....

....

....

What challenged me today and how can I shift my thinking tomorrow?

....

....

....

SELF CARE

I took care of myself today by...

....

....

....

I drank ☐ glasses of water today

ON A SCALE OF 1 TO 10, HOW DID I DO TODAY?

THRIVING 10

9

8

7

6

5

4

3

2

1 SURVIVING

Today I am at a ☐

REMEMBER

An hour before I go to bed, I will put my work aside (and my phone), breathe and set my intention for tomorrow.

It's a new day!

MORNING PRACTICE

My INTENTION for today is...

....

....

....

I am THANKFUL for...

....

....

....

Navigate through the noise and simply FOCUS on three to-do's:

1 ....

2 ....

3 ....

Welcome today and RELEASE....

....

....

....

AFTERNOON PRACTICE

I LISTENED to...

....

....

....

I RELATED and CONNECTED to...

....

....

....

I CELEBRATED...

....

....

....

What challenged me today and how can I shift my thinking tomorrow?

....

....

....

SELF CARE

I took care of myself today by...

....

....

I drank [   ] glasses of water today

ON A SCALE OF 1 TO 10, HOW DID I DO TODAY?

THRIVING 10

9

8

7

6

5

4

3

2

1 SURVIVING

Today I am at a [   ]

REMEMBER

An hour before I go to bed, I will put my work aside (and my phone), breathe and set my intention for tomorrow.

It's a new day!

TODAY'S MINDFUL TIP

Need a reboot? We all do in certain parts of our lives. The notion that if things are going in the wrong direction they cannot be reversed is NOT TRUE. Every single moment we get the chance to begin again. Let's hit the mental pause button and get off the autopilot path we are on.

MORNING PRACTICE

My INTENTION for today is...

....

....

....

I am THANKFUL for...

....

....

....

Navigate through the noise and simply FOCUS on three to-do's:

1 ....

2 ....

3 ....

Welcome today and RELEASE....

....

....

....

AFTERNOON PRACTICE

I LISTENED to...

....

....

....

I RELATED and CONNECTED to...

....

....

....

I CELEBRATED...

....

....

....

What challenged me today and how can I shift my thinking tomorrow?

....

....

....

SELF CARE

I took care of myself today by...

....

....

....

I drank ☐ glasses of water today

ON A SCALE OF 1 TO 10, HOW DID I DO TODAY?

THRIVING 10
9
8
7
6
5
4
3
2
1 SURVIVING

Today I am at a ☐

REMEMBER

An hour before I go to bed, I will put my work aside (and my phone), breathe and set my intention for tomorrow.

It's a new day!

TODAY'S MINDFUL TIP

Bring boldness into your life today. Research indicates that the moments we are most proud of are those when we let go of the drama that our irrational fears so often create so we can...face uncertainty and discomfort with confidence and conviction and do something for others with no need for reward or recognition.

MORNING PRACTICE

My INTENTION for today is...

....
....
....

I am THANKFUL for...

....
....
....

Navigate through the noise and simply FOCUS on three to-do's:

1 ....

2 ....

3 ....

Welcome today and RELEASE....

....
....
....

AFTERNOON PRACTICE

I LISTENED to...

_____

_____

_____

I RELATED and CONNECTED to...

_____

_____

_____

I CELEBRATED...

_____

_____

_____

What challenged me today and how can I shift my thinking tomorrow?

_____

_____

_____

SELF CARE

I took care of myself today by...

_____

_____

I drank ☐ glasses of water today

ON A SCALE OF 1 TO 10, HOW DID I DO TODAY?

THRIVING 10

9

8

7

6

5

4

3

2

1 SURVIVING

Today I am at a ☐

REMEMBER

An hour before I go to bed, I will put my work aside (and my phone), breathe and set my intention for tomorrow.

It's a new day!

TODAY'S MINDFUL TIP

Do more things that make you forget to check your electronic devices. What if we all found a way to get away for a few minutes or more each day without our beloved devices? When we are engaged and energized by our actions and excited to slow down and listen, we tend to forget about the instant gratification we get from our technology.

MORNING PRACTICE

My INTENTION for today is...

....

....

....

I am THANKFUL for...

....

....

....

Navigate through the noise and simply FOCUS on three to-do's:

1 ....

2 ....

3 ....

Welcome today and RELEASE....

....

....

....

AFTERNOON PRACTICE

I LISTENED to...

....

....

....

I RELATED and CONNECTED to...

....

....

....

I CELEBRATED...

....

....

....

What challenged me today and how can I shift my thinking tomorrow?

....

....

....

SELF CARE

I took care of myself today by...

....

....

....

I drank ☐ glasses of water today

ON A SCALE OF 1 TO 10, HOW DID I DO TODAY?

THRIVING 10

9

8

7

6

5

4

3

2

1 SURVIVING

Today I am at a ☐

REMEMBER

An hour before I go to bed, I will put my work aside (and my phone), breathe and set my intention for tomorrow.

It's a new day!

TODAY'S MINDFUL TIP

Stop trying to change people. You will save so much time and energy.

MORNING PRACTICE

My INTENTION for today is...

....

....

....

I am THANKFUL for...

....

....

....

Navigate through the noise and simply FOCUS on three to-do's:

1 ....

2 ....

3 ....

Welcome today and RELEASE....

....

....

....

AFTERNOON PRACTICE

I LISTENED to...

_____

_____

_____

I RELATED and CONNECTED to...

_____

_____

_____

I CELEBRATED...

_____

_____

_____

What challenged me today and how can I shift my thinking tomorrow?

_____

_____

SELF CARE

I took care of myself today by...

_____

_____

I drank ☐ glasses of water today

ON A SCALE OF
1 TO 10, HOW DID
I DO TODAY?

THRIVING 10
9
8
7
6
5
4
3
2
1 SURVIVING

Today I am at a ☐

REMEMBER

An hour before I go to bed, I will put my work aside (and my phone), breathe and set my intention for tomorrow.

DAY 157

It's a new day!

We are born with amazing imaginations, but it often gets hijacked by our limiting beliefs. Today, think deeply and explore your ideas. Creativity isn't a switch that's flipped on and off. It's a way of seeing, engaging with and responding to the world around us.

MORNING PRACTICE

My INTENTION for today is...

....
....
....

I am THANKFUL for...

....
....
....

Navigate through the noise and simply FOCUS on three to-do's:

1 ....

2 ....

3 ....

Welcome today and RELEASE....

....
....
....

AFTERNOON PRACTICE

I LISTENED to...

....

....

....

I RELATED and CONNECTED to...

....

....

....

I CELEBRATED...

....

....

....

What challenged me today and how can I shift my thinking tomorrow?

....

....

....

SELF CARE

I took care of myself today by...

....

....

....

I drank ⬚ glasses of water today

ON A SCALE OF 1 TO 10, HOW DID I DO TODAY?

↑

THRIVING 10

9

8

7

6

5

4

3

2

1 SURVIVING

Today I am at a ⬚

REMEMBER

An hour before I go to bed, I will put my work aside (and my phone), breathe and set my intention for tomorrow.

It's a new day!

MORNING PRACTICE

My INTENTION for today is...

....

....

....

I am THANKFUL for...

....

....

....

Navigate through the noise and simply FOCUS on three to-do's:

1 ....

2 ....

3 ....

Welcome today and RELEASE....

....

....

....

TODAY'S MINDFUL TIP

Listen to your body and breathe, it's usually right!

AFTERNOON PRACTICE

I LISTENED to...

....

....

....

I RELATED and CONNECTED to...

....

....

....

I CELEBRATED...

....

....

....

What challenged me today and how can I shift my thinking tomorrow?

....

....

....

SELF CARE

I took care of myself today by...

....

....

....

I drank ☐ glasses of water today

ON A SCALE OF 1 TO 10, HOW DID I DO TODAY?

THRIVING 10

9

8

7

6

5

4

3

2

1 SURVIVING

Today I am at a ☐

REMEMBER

An hour before I go to bed, I will put my work aside (and my phone), breathe and set my intention for tomorrow.

DAY 159

It's a new day!

TODAY'S MINDFUL TIP

An important conversation deserves face time. Email or texting can often lead to assumptions and mistakes. Talking face-to-face can save time and the chance of being misunderstood.

MORNING PRACTICE

My INTENTION for today is...

....
....
....

I am THANKFUL for...

....
....
....

Navigate through the noise and simply FOCUS on three to-do's:

1 ....

2 ....

3 ....

Welcome today and RELEASE....

....
....
....

AFTERNOON PRACTICE

I LISTENED to...

....

....

....

I RELATED and CONNECTED to...

....

....

....

I CELEBRATED...

....

....

....

What challenged me today and how can I shift my thinking tomorrow?

....

....

....

SELF CARE

I took care of myself today by...

....

....

I drank ☐ glasses of water today

ON A SCALE OF 1 TO 10, HOW DID I DO TODAY?

THRIVING 10
9
8
7
6
5
4
3
2
1 SURVIVING

Today I am at a ☐

REMEMBER

An hour before I go to bed, I will put my work aside (and my phone), breathe and set my intention for tomorrow.

It's a new day!

TODAY'S MINDFUL TIP

Choose often and choose well. Instead of doing everything, do the things that matter most to you.

MORNING PRACTICE

My INTENTION for today is...

....

....

....

I am THANKFUL for...

....

....

....

Navigate through the noise and simply FOCUS on three to-do's:

1 ....

2 ....

3 ....

Welcome today and RELEASE....

....

....

....

AFTERNOON PRACTICE

I LISTENED to...

....

....

....

I RELATED and CONNECTED to...

....

....

....

I CELEBRATED...

....

....

....

What challenged me today and how can I shift my thinking tomorrow?

....

....

....

SELF CARE

I took care of myself today by...

....

....

....

I drank ☐ glasses of water today

ON A SCALE OF 1 TO 10, HOW DID I DO TODAY?

THRIVING 10

9

8

7

6

5

4

3

2

1 SURVIVING

Today I am at a ☐

REMEMBER

An hour before I go to bed, I will put my work aside (and my phone), breathe and set my intention for tomorrow.

It's a new day!

MORNING PRACTICE

My INTENTION for today is...

....

....

....

I am THANKFUL for...

....

....

....

Navigate through the noise and simply FOCUS on three to-do's:

1 ....

2 ....

3 ....

Welcome today and RELEASE....

....

....

....

AFTERNOON PRACTICE

I LISTENED to...

....

....

....

I RELATED and CONNECTED to...

....

....

....

I CELEBRATED...

....

....

....

What challenged me today and how can I shift my thinking tomorrow?

....

....

....

SELF CARE

I took care of myself today by...

....

....

....

I drank ☐ glasses of water today

ON A SCALE OF 1 TO 10, HOW DID I DO TODAY?

THRIVING 10
9
8
7
6
5
4
3
2
1 SURVIVING

Today I am at a ☐

REMEMBER

An hour before I go to bed, I will put my work aside (and my phone), breathe and set my intention for tomorrow.

DAY 162

It's a new day!

TODAY'S MINDFUL TIP

"Be kind, for everyone you meet is fighting a hard battle."
—Socrates

MORNING PRACTICE

My INTENTION for today is...

....

....

....

I am THANKFUL for...

....

....

....

Navigate through the noise and simply FOCUS on three to-do's:

1 ....

2 ....

3 ....

Welcome today and RELEASE....

....

....

....

AFTERNOON PRACTICE

I LISTENED to...

....

....

....

I RELATED and CONNECTED to...

....

....

....

I CELEBRATED...

....

....

....

What challenged me today and how can I shift my thinking tomorrow?

....

....

....

SELF CARE

I took care of myself today by...

....

....

I drank ☐ glasses of water today

ON A SCALE OF 1 TO 10, HOW DID I DO TODAY?

↑

THRIVING 10
9
8
7
6
5
4
3
2
1 SURVIVING

Today I am at a ☐

REMEMBER

An hour before I go to bed, I will put my work aside (and my phone), breathe and set my intention for tomorrow.

DAY 163

It's a new day!

TODAY'S MINDFUL TIP

It's dumpster day.
Pick one day a week to throw out your head trash. Once it is gone resist the urge to go dumpster diving!

MORNING PRACTICE

My **INTENTION** for today is...

....
....
....

I am **THANKFUL** for...

....
....
....

Navigate through the noise and simply **FOCUS** on three to-do's:

1 ....

2 ....

3 ....

Welcome today and **RELEASE**....

....
....
....

AFTERNOON PRACTICE

I LISTENED to...

....

....

....

I RELATED and CONNECTED to...

....

....

....

I CELEBRATED...

....

....

....

What challenged me today and how can I shift my thinking tomorrow?

....

....

....

SELF CARE

I took care of myself today by...

....

....

....

I drank ☐ glasses of water today

ON A SCALE OF 1 TO 10, HOW DID I DO TODAY?

THRIVING 10

9

8

7

6

5

4

3

2

1 SURVIVING

Today I am at a ☐

REMEMBER

An hour before I go to bed, I will put my work aside (and my phone), breathe and set my intention for tomorrow.

It's a new day!

TODAY'S MINDFUL TIP

Do you hear what I hear? Take three minutes and listen to the sounds that surround you. Note the sounds you hear and where they are coming from. When we practice mindful listening we activate the Reticular Activating System in the brain. The more we practice, the easier it is for us to use it in our daily lives.

MORNING PRACTICE

My INTENTION for today is...

....

....

....

I am THANKFUL for...

....

....

....

Navigate through the noise and simply FOCUS on three to-do's:

1 ....

2 ....

3 ....

Welcome today and RELEASE....

....

....

....

AFTERNOON PRACTICE

I LISTENED to...

....

....

....

I RELATED and CONNECTED to...

....

....

....

I CELEBRATED...

....

....

....

What challenged me today and how can I shift my thinking tomorrow?

....

....

....

SELF CARE

I took care of myself today by...

....

....

....

I drank ☐ glasses of water today

ON A SCALE OF 1 TO 10, HOW DID I DO TODAY?

↑

THRIVING 10

9

8

7

6

5

4

3

2

1 SURVIVING

Today I am at a ☐

REMEMBER

An hour before I go to bed, I will put my work aside (and my phone), breathe and set my intention for tomorrow.

It's a new day!

TODAY'S MINDFUL TIP

Show the people you are closest with how much you appreciate them in your life. Sometimes we take for granted what we have every day.

MORNING PRACTICE

My INTENTION for today is...

....

....

....

I am THANKFUL for...

....

....

....

Navigate through the noise and simply FOCUS on three to-do's:

1 ....

2 ....

3 ....

Welcome today and RELEASE....

....

....

....

AFTERNOON PRACTICE

I LISTENED to...

....

....

....

I RELATED and CONNECTED to...

....

....

....

I CELEBRATED...

....

....

....

What challenged me today and how can I shift my thinking tomorrow?

....

....

....

SELF CARE

I took care of myself today by...

....

....

I drank ☐ glasses of water today

ON A SCALE OF 1 TO 10, HOW DID I DO TODAY?

THRIVING 10

9

8

7

6

5

4

3

2

1 SURVIVING

Today I am at a ☐

REMEMBER

An hour before I go to bed, I will put my work aside (and my phone), breathe and set my intention for tomorrow.

DAY 166

It's a new day!

TODAY'S MINDFUL TIP

"To begin, begin."
—William Wordsworth

Today is the day to start that one thing we have been putting off. So often we get stuck by overthinking the process instead of just jumping into it. Picture the end result and how good you will feel. Release your anxiety by remembering that we get past procrastination by taking one step at a time, locking in our goals and STARTING.

MORNING PRACTICE

My INTENTION for today is...

....
....
....

I am THANKFUL for...

....
....
....

Navigate through the noise and simply FOCUS on three to-do's:

1 ....

2 ....

3 ....

Welcome today and RELEASE....

....
....
....

AFTERNOON PRACTICE

I LISTENED to...

_____

_____

_____

I RELATED and CONNECTED to...

_____

_____

_____

I CELEBRATED...

_____

_____

_____

What challenged me today and how can I shift my thinking tomorrow?

_____

_____

_____

SELF CARE

I took care of myself today by...

_____

_____

I drank [ ] glasses of water today

ON A SCALE OF
1 TO 10, HOW DID
I DO TODAY?

THRIVING 10

9

8

7

6

5

4

3

2

1 SURVIVING

Today I am at a [ ]

REMEMBER

An hour before I go to bed,
I will put my work aside
(and my phone), breathe
and set my intention for
tomorrow.

DAY 167

It's a new day!

TODAY'S MINDFUL TIP

"Remember there's no such thing as a small act of kindness. Every act creates a ripple with no logical end."
—Scott Adams

MORNING PRACTICE

My INTENTION for today is...

....

....

....

I am THANKFUL for...

....

....

....

Navigate through the noise and simply FOCUS on three to-do's:

1 ....

2 ....

3 ....

Welcome today and RELEASE....

....

....

....

AFTERNOON PRACTICE

I LISTENED to...

_____

_____

_____

I RELATED and CONNECTED to...

_____

_____

_____

I CELEBRATED...

_____

_____

_____

What challenged me today and how can I shift my thinking tomorrow?

_____

_____

_____

SELF CARE

I took care of myself today by...

_____

_____

_____

I drank ☐ glasses of water today

ON A SCALE OF 1 TO 10, HOW DID I DO TODAY?

↑
THRIVING   10
9
8
7
6
5
4
3
2
1   SURVIVING

Today I am at a ☐

REMEMBER

An hour before I go to bed, I will put my work aside (and my phone), breathe and set my intention for tomorrow.

It's a new day!

TODAY'S
MINDFUL TIP

Will you commit to giving yourself some quality down time today? Quality trumps quantity. Even five minutes in absolute solitude without your phone or any other distractions will work. If you want to truly connect with others, you need to connect with yourself first.

MORNING PRACTICE

My INTENTION for today is...

....

....

....

I am THANKFUL for...

....

....

....

Navigate through the noise and simply FOCUS on three to-do's:

1 ....

2 ....

3 ....

Welcome today and RELEASE....

....

....

....

AFTERNOON PRACTICE

I LISTENED to...

....

....

....

I RELATED and CONNECTED to...

....

....

....

I CELEBRATED...

....

....

....

What challenged me today and how can I shift my thinking tomorrow?

....

....

....

SELF CARE

I took care of myself today by...

....

....

....

I drank ☐ glasses of water today

ON A SCALE OF 1 TO 10, HOW DID I DO TODAY?

THRIVING 10
9
8
7
6
5
4
3
2
1 SURVIVING

Today I am at a ☐

REMEMBER

An hour before I go to bed, I will put my work aside (and my phone), breathe and set my intention for tomorrow.

It's a new day!

TODAY'S
MINDFUL TIP

Be somebody who
makes everybody feel
like a somebody.
—Kid President

MORNING PRACTICE

My INTENTION for today is...

....

....

....

I am THANKFUL for...

....

....

....

Navigate through the noise and simply FOCUS on
three to-do's:

1 ....

2 ....

3 ....

Welcome today and RELEASE....

....

....

....

AFTERNOON PRACTICE

I LISTENED to...

....

....

....

I RELATED and CONNECTED to...

....

....

....

I CELEBRATED...

....

....

....

What challenged me today and how can I shift my thinking tomorrow?

....

....

....

SELF CARE

I took care of myself today by...

....

....

....

I drank ☐ glasses of water today

ON A SCALE OF 1 TO 10, HOW DID I DO TODAY?

↑

THRIVING 10

9

8

7

6

5

4

3

2

1 SURVIVING

Today I am at a ☐

REMEMBER

An hour before I go to bed, I will put my work aside (and my phone), breathe and set my intention for tomorrow.

It's a new day!

Describe a time when you felt most alive and engaged at school? Jot the experience down in detail and look for who was involved, what you were doing and how you showed up that day.

MORNING PRACTICE

My INTENTION for today is...

....

....

....

I am THANKFUL for...

....

....

....

Navigate through the noise and simply FOCUS on three to-do's:

1 ....

2 ....

3 ....

Welcome today and RELEASE....

....

....

....

AFTERNOON PRACTICE

I LISTENED to...

....

....

....

I RELATED and CONNECTED to...

....

....

....

I CELEBRATED...

....

....

....

What challenged me today and how can I shift my thinking tomorrow?

....

....

....

SELF CARE

I took care of myself today by...

....

....

....

I drank [   ] glasses of water today

ON A SCALE OF 1 TO 10, HOW DID I DO TODAY?

THRIVING 10

9

8

7

6

5

4

3

2

1 SURVIVING

Today I am at a [   ]

REMEMBER

An hour before I go to bed, I will put my work aside (and my phone), breathe and set my intention for tomorrow.

It's a new day!

MORNING PRACTICE

My INTENTION for today is...

....
....
....

I am THANKFUL for...

....
....
....

Navigate through the noise and simply FOCUS on
three to-do's:

1 ....

2 ....

3 ....

Welcome today and RELEASE....

....
....
....

AFTERNOON PRACTICE

I LISTENED to...

....

....

....

I RELATED and CONNECTED to...

....

....

....

I CELEBRATED...

....

....

....

What challenged me today and how can I shift my thinking tomorrow?

....

....

....

SELF CARE

I took care of myself today by...

....

....

....

I drank ☐ glasses of water today

ON A SCALE OF
I TO 10, HOW DID
I DO TODAY?

↑

THRIVING 10

9

8

7

6

5

4

3

2

1   SURVIVING

Today I am at a ☐

REMEMBER

An hour before I go to bed,
I will put my work aside
(and my phone), breathe
and set my intention for
tomorrow.

DAY 172

It's a new day!

TODAY'S MINDFUL TIP

Approach life with a vulnerable heart and an instinct to do not necessarily what is expected, but what is "right" for kids.

MORNING PRACTICE

My INTENTION for today is...

....

....

....

I am THANKFUL for...

....

....

....

Navigate through the noise and simply FOCUS on three to-do's:

1 ....

2 ....

3 ....

Welcome today and RELEASE....

....

....

....

AFTERNOON PRACTICE

I LISTENED to...

....

....

....

I RELATED and CONNECTED to...

....

....

....

I CELEBRATED...

....

....

....

What challenged me today and how can I shift my thinking tomorrow?

....

....

....

SELF CARE

I took care of myself today by...

....

....

....

I drank ☐ glasses of water today

ON A SCALE OF 1 TO 10, HOW DID I DO TODAY?

THRIVING 10

9

8

7

6

5

4

3

2

1 SURVIVING

Today I am at a ☐

REMEMBER

An hour before I go to bed, I will put my work aside (and my phone), breathe and set my intention for tomorrow.

It's a new day!

MORNING PRACTICE

My INTENTION for today is...

....

....

....

I am THANKFUL for...

....

....

....

Navigate through the noise and simply FOCUS on three to-do's:

1 ....

2 ....

3 ....

Welcome today and RELEASE....

....

....

....

AFTERNOON PRACTICE

I LISTENED to...

....

....

....

I RELATED and CONNECTED to...

....

....

....

I CELEBRATED...

....

....

....

What challenged me today and how can I shift my thinking tomorrow?

....

....

....

SELF CARE

I took care of myself today by...

....

....

....

I drank ☐ glasses of water today

ON A SCALE OF 1 TO 10, HOW DID I DO TODAY?

THRIVING 10

9

8

7

6

5

4

3

2

1 SURVIVING

Today I am at a ☐

REMEMBER

An hour before I go to bed, I will put my work aside (and my phone), breathe and set my intention for tomorrow.

It's a new day!

TODAY'S MINDFUL TIP

Disrupt the status quo with kindness. Today, think "big", embrace challenges and create opportunities for kids to thrive.

MORNING PRACTICE

My INTENTION for today is...

....

....

....

I am THANKFUL for...

....

....

....

Navigate through the noise and simply FOCUS on three to-do's:

1 ....

2 ....

3 ....

Welcome today and RELEASE....

....

....

....

AFTERNOON PRACTICE

I LISTENED to...

....

....

....

I RELATED and CONNECTED to...

....

....

....

I CELEBRATED...

....

....

....

What challenged me today and how can I shift my thinking tomorrow?

....

....

....

SELF CARE

I took care of myself today by...

....

....

....

I drank ☐ glasses of water today

ON A SCALE OF 1 TO 10, HOW DID I DO TODAY?

THRIVING 10
9
8
7
6
5
4
3
2
1 SURVIVING

Today I am at a ☐

REMEMBER

An hour before I go to bed, I will put my work aside (and my phone), breathe and set my intention for tomorrow.

Resilience Reflection

EMOTIONAL RESILIENCE IS...

a person's ability to recover after a setback and to thrive in the midst of challenges, not just survive.

CHECK IN

Reflecting on the last 25 days, how well did I implement my daily practices (*before school, after school, self-care, mindfulness*)?

What went WELL?

....

....

....

....

What did I STRUGGLE with?

....

....

....

....

ON ANY GIVEN DAY we experience a myriad of highs and lows. While some emotional resilience comes naturally to us, we all have the ability to increase our capacity over time and thrive.

Look back on the past 25 days. On a scale of 1 to 10, where do I FIND MYSELF on this line? *Add up your daily scores and divide by 25 to indicate your score.* I AM a ☐

1 2 3 4 5 6 7 8 9 10 →

SURVIVING   THRIVING

What ADJUSTMENTS can I make for the next 25 days to THRIVE?

....
....
....
....

Keep Going!
You've Got This!

MY THOUGHTS TODAY...

It's a new day!

TODAY'S MINDFUL TIP

The name game.
Naming our emotional experiences helps us separate the experience from ourselves. Research shows that when we can name a problem, we calm our brain instead of getting swept up in it.

MORNING PRACTICE

My INTENTION for today is...

....
....
....

I am THANKFUL for...

....
....
....

Navigate through the noise and simply FOCUS on three to-do's:

1 ....

2 ....

3 ....

Welcome today and RELEASE....

....
....
....

AFTERNOON PRACTICE

I LISTENED to...

....

....

....

I RELATED and CONNECTED to...

....

....

....

I CELEBRATED...

....

....

....

What challenged me today and how can I shift my thinking tomorrow?

....

....

....

SELF CARE

I took care of myself today by...

....

....

....

I drank ☐ glasses of water today

ON A SCALE OF 1 TO 10, HOW DID I DO TODAY?

THRIVING 10
          9
          8
          7
          6
          5
          4
          3
          2
          1 SURVIVING

Today I am at a ☐

REMEMBER

An hour before I go to bed, I will put my work aside (and my phone), breathe and set my intention for tomorrow.

It's a new day!

MORNING PRACTICE

My INTENTION for today is...

....

....

....

I am THANKFUL for...

....

....

....

Navigate through the noise and simply FOCUS on three to-do's:

1 ....

2 ....

3 ....

Welcome today and RELEASE....

....

....

....

TODAY'S MINDFUL TIP

We live in a world of change and uncertainty and if we want our kids to be an integral part of the future we need to lead with courageous compassion.

AFTERNOON PRACTICE

I LISTENED to...

....

....

....

I RELATED and CONNECTED to...

....

....

....

I CELEBRATED...

....

....

....

What challenged me today and how can I shift my thinking tomorrow?

....

....

....

SELF CARE

I took care of myself today by...

....

....

....

I drank ☐ glasses of water today

ON A SCALE OF 1 TO 10, HOW DID I DO TODAY?

THRIVING 10

9

8

7

6

5

4

3

2

1 SURVIVING

Today I am at a ☐

REMEMBER

An hour before I go to bed, I will put my work aside (and my phone), breathe and set my intention for tomorrow.

It's a new day!

MORNING PRACTICE

My INTENTION for today is...

....

....

....

I am THANKFUL for...

....

....

....

Navigate through the noise and simply FOCUS on three to-do's:

1 ....

2 ....

3 ....

Welcome today and RELEASE....

....

....

....

AFTERNOON PRACTICE

I LISTENED to...

....

....

....

I RELATED and CONNECTED to...

....

....

....

I CELEBRATED...

....

....

....

What challenged me today and how can I shift my thinking tomorrow?

....

....

....

SELF CARE

I took care of myself today by...

....

....

....

I drank ☐ glasses of water today

ON A SCALE OF 1 TO 10, HOW DID I DO TODAY?

THRIVING 10

9

8

7

6

5

4

3

2

1 SURVIVING

Today I am at a ☐

REMEMBER

An hour before I go to bed, I will put my work aside (and my phone), breathe and set my intention for tomorrow.

It's a new day!

TODAY'S MINDFUL TIP

If reality is 90% perception, let's consider the best instead of the worst! Give yourself and others a break. Just imagine, perhaps, that it is not about you, and no one is out to get you. Use patience and compassion today to combat judgment.

MORNING PRACTICE

My INTENTION for today is...

....

....

....

I am THANKFUL for...

....

....

....

Navigate through the noise and simply FOCUS on three to-do's:

1 ....

2 ....

3 ....

Welcome today and RELEASE....

....

....

....

AFTERNOON PRACTICE

I LISTENED to...

....

....

....

I RELATED and CONNECTED to...

....

....

....

I CELEBRATED...

....

....

....

What challenged me today and how can I shift my thinking tomorrow?

....

....

....

SELF CARE

I took care of myself today by...

....

....

....

I drank [ ] glasses of water today

ON A SCALE OF 1 TO 10, HOW DID I DO TODAY?

THRIVING 10
9
8
7
6
5
4
3
2
1 SURVIVING

Today I am at a [ ]

REMEMBER

An hour before I go to bed, I will put my work aside (and my phone), breathe and set my intention for tomorrow.

It's a new day!

TODAY'S MINDFUL TIP

Approach today with "what happened" instead of "what's wrong".

MORNING PRACTICE

My INTENTION for today is...

....
....
....

I am THANKFUL for...

....
....
....

Navigate through the noise and simply FOCUS on three to-do's:

1 ....

2 ....

3 ....

Welcome today and RELEASE....

....
....
....

AFTERNOON PRACTICE

I **LISTENED** to...

_____

_____

_____

I **RELATED** and **CONNECTED** to...

_____

_____

_____

I **CELEBRATED**...

_____

_____

_____

What challenged me today and how can I shift my thinking tomorrow?

_____

_____

_____

SELF CARE

I took care of myself today by...

_____

_____

_____

I drank ☐ glasses of water today

ON A SCALE OF 1 TO 10, HOW DID I DO TODAY?

THRIVING 10
9
8
7
6
5
4
3
2
1 SURVIVING

Today I am at a ☐

REMEMBER

An hour before I go to bed, I will put my work aside (and my phone), breathe and set my intention for tomorrow.

It's a new day!

TODAY'S MINDFUL TIP

"Whether you think you can, or you think you can't – you're right."
—Henry Ford
Part of getting what you want in life is believing you can have it. As human beings, we are wired to follow what we think and what we believe. Think positive.

MORNING PRACTICE

My INTENTION for today is...

....

....

....

I am THANKFUL for...

....

....

....

Navigate through the noise and simply FOCUS on three to-do's:

1 ....

2 ....

3 ....

Welcome today and RELEASE....

....

....

....

AFTERNOON PRACTICE

I LISTENED to...

....

....

....

I RELATED and CONNECTED to...

....

....

....

I CELEBRATED...

....

....

....

What challenged me today and how can I shift my thinking tomorrow?

....

....

....

SELF CARE

I took care of myself today by...

....

....

....

I drank ☐ glasses of water today

ON A SCALE OF 1 TO 10, HOW DID I DO TODAY?

THRIVING 10

9

8

7

6

5

4

3

2

1 SURVIVING

Today I am at a ☐

REMEMBER

An hour before I go to bed, I will put my work aside (and my phone), breathe and set my intention for tomorrow.

It's a new day!

TODAY'S
MINDFUL TIP

Ordinary is
extraordinary!
Be thankful for the
ordinary routine things
in life. They are gifts.

MORNING PRACTICE

My INTENTION for today is...

....

....

....

I am THANKFUL for...

....

....

....

Navigate through the noise and simply FOCUS on three to-do's:

1 ....

2 ....

3 ....

Welcome today and RELEASE....

....

....

....

AFTERNOON PRACTICE

I **LISTENED** to...

....

....

....

I **RELATED** and **CONNECTED** to...

....

....

....

I **CELEBRATED**...

....

....

....

What challenged me today and how can I shift my thinking tomorrow?

....

....

....

SELF CARE

I took care of myself today by...

....

....

....

I drank [ ] glasses of water today

ON A SCALE OF 1 TO 10, HOW DID I DO TODAY?

THRIVING 10

9

8

7

6

5

4

3

2

1 SURVIVING

Today I am at a [ ]

REMEMBER

An hour before I go to bed, I will put my work aside (and my phone), breathe and set my intention for tomorrow.

It's a new day!

TODAY'S
MINDFUL TIP

What do I want my
legacy to be? Are my
daily actions living up to
my legacy?

MORNING PRACTICE

My INTENTION for today is...

....

....

....

I am THANKFUL for...

....

....

....

Navigate through the noise and simply FOCUS on three to-do's:

1 ....

2 ....

3 ....

Welcome today and RELEASE....

....

....

....

AFTERNOON PRACTICE

I LISTENED to...

_____

_____

_____

I RELATED and CONNECTED to...

_____

_____

_____

I CELEBRATED...

_____

_____

_____

What challenged me today and how can I shift my thinking tomorrow?

_____

_____

_____

SELF CARE

I took care of myself today by...

_____

_____

_____

I drank ☐ glasses of water today

ON A SCALE OF 1 TO 10, HOW DID I DO TODAY?

↑

THRIVING 10

9

8

7

6

5

4

3

2

1   SURVIVING

Today I am at a ☐

REMEMBER

An hour before I go to bed, I will put my work aside (and my phone), breathe and set my intention for tomorrow.

DAY 184

It's a new day!

TODAY'S MINDFUL TIP

"May you be proud of the work you do, the person you are, and the difference you make."
—Author unknown

MORNING PRACTICE

My INTENTION for today is...

....

....

....

I am THANKFUL for...

....

....

....

Navigate through the noise and simply FOCUS on three to-do's:

1 ....

2 ....

3 ....

Welcome today and RELEASE....

....

....

....

AFTERNOON PRACTICE

I LISTENED to...

_____

_____

_____

I RELATED and CONNECTED to...

_____

_____

_____

I CELEBRATED...

_____

_____

_____

What challenged me today and how can I shift my thinking tomorrow?

_____

_____

_____

SELF CARE

I took care of myself today by...

_____

_____

_____

I drank ☐ glasses of water today

ON A SCALE OF 1 TO 10, HOW DID I DO TODAY?

THRIVING 10

9

8

7

6

5

4

3

2

1 SURVIVING

Today I am at a ☐

REMEMBER

An hour before I go to bed, I will put my work aside (and my phone), breathe and set my intention for tomorrow.

Resilience Reflection

EMOTIONAL RESILIENCE IS...

a person's ability to recover after a setback and to thrive in the midst of challenges, not just survive.

FINAL CHECK IN

Reflecting on the SCHOOL YEAR, how well did I implement my daily practices (*before school, after school, self-care, mindfulness*)?

What went WELL?

....
....
....
....

What did I STRUGGLE with?

....
....
....
....

ON ANY GIVEN DAY we experience a myriad of highs and lows. While some emotional resilience comes naturally to us, we all have the ability to increase our capacity over time and thrive.

Look back on the past resilience reflection pages (DAY 25, 50, 75, 100, 125, 150, 175). On a scale of 1 to 10, where do I FIND MYSELF on this line? *Add up your resilience reflection scores above and divide by 7 to indicate your score.* I AM a ☐

1   2   3   4   5   6   7   8   9   10

SURVIVING   THRIVING

What ADJUSTMENTS can I make for the next school year to THRIVE?

....

....

....

....

Way to go! You Did It!

MY THOUGHTS TODAY...

_____

_____

_____

_____

_____

_____

_____

_____

_____

_____

_____

_____

Kami Guarino

Kami Guarino is a mom of four unique learners and a wife, educator, leader, mentor, and friend. She has worked with and been inspired by some of the most talented and insightful people throughout her career in education. Yet so often these individuals who have served others while striving to make a difference in the world feel defeated, exhausted, and ineffective. Kami is committed to shifting an educator's mindset from surviving to thriving.

Kami is an educational leadership consultant and founder of The Excellence Team. During her thirty-year journey in the K–12 education system, she has experienced many personal and professional highs and lows. Her background in counseling and school leadership—combined with extensive experience in mindfulness, restorative practices, and trauma-informed care—has naturally led her to focus on the whole child/whole adult approach to education.

Outside of the education world, Kami spends most of her time with her husband of twenty-seven years and her four kids, who are sprinkled throughout the world. She loves the outdoors, family traditions, traveling, and keeping her mind and body fit.

Let's Work Together

You can continue to ignite a shift in your school by using Kami and The Excellence Team through their revolutionary out-of-the-box professional development programs.

Interactive and Collaborative Workshops:

Our goal is to provide you with personalized professional development that will connect and ignite your teachers, staff and administration to think differently and be part of an exceptional organization.

Together we will assess the needs of your building and identify common trends. Workshop topics include:

- Create a community for inspired growth and leadership.
- Embrace our cultural differences while celebrating our individual strengths.
- Craft a social emotional approach to learn and lead.
- Cultivate resilience, mindfulness and wellness.
- Be intentional and have a part of schoolwide decision making.

In addition, Kami offers online courses and coaching.

For more details please contact Kami at Kami@TheExcellenceTeam.net or visit their website at TheExcellenceTeam.net.

THE EXCELLENCE TEAM